The Naked Educator

How to Survive in the Middle Kingdom

Francisca Epale

© 2016 BY FRANCISCA EPALE

ALL RIGHTS RESERVED. NO PART OF THIS PUBLICATION MAY BE REPRODUCED, DISTRIBUTED, OR TRANSMITTED IN ANY FORM OR BY ANY MEANS, INCLUDING PHOTOCOPYING, RECORDING, OR OTHER ELECTRONIC OR MECHANICAL METHODS, WITHOUT PRIOR WRITTEN PERMISSION OF THE PUBLISHER, EXCEPT FOR THE USE OF BRIEF QUOTATIONS IN A BOOK REVIEW.

PRINTED IN CANADA
ISBN: 978-1-77277-058-2

10-10-10 PUBLISHING
MARKHAM, ONTARIO
CANADA

Contents

Gratitude	vii
Accolades	xi
About the Author	xv
Foreword	xvii
Chapter 1: The Genesis	1
Chapter 2: Why I Went to the Middle Kingdom	3
Chapter 3: Language and Culture	11
Chapter 4: Teaching in the Middle Kingdom	19
Chapter 5: Success Stories	33
Chapter 6: Character-Building Experiences	47
Chapter 7: The Power of Faith	61
Chapter 8: What I Liked about the Middle Kingdom	71
Chapter 9: Life Lessons Learned	81
Chapter 10: Suggestions for Surviving in the Middle Kingdom	91
References	105

DEDICATION

My book, *The Naked Educator: How to Survive in the Middle Kingdom*, is dedicated to my parents who are in heaven: the late Dr. Simon Joseph Epale and the late Tessa Eunice Epale. The dedication is also for my nuclear and extended family members.

GRATITUDE

No nonfiction writer works alone and this book is no exception. My heartfelt appreciation goes to the following people: my brother, Priso Epale, who encouraged me to go to China to teach English. Dr. Jim Pellegrini and Kat Ostroumova, Director and Director of International Operations at TESOL Global College, respectively – who both taught me a TESOL course and guaranteed me an overseas job upon completion.

I would also like to thank three special people whose book-writing programs helped me write my first book in a timely manner: Brian Tracy, for his program *How to Write a Book and Become a Published Author*; Arel Moodie, for his *True Speaking Success* program, which includes *How to Write Your Own Book*; and also Raymond Aaron's *Get Your Book Done* 3-day boot camp.

Thank you Noel Walrond, President of My Dreams Work, Inc., and author of *There is No Tomorrow, The Ultimate Guide to Beating Procrastination*. You helped me through your 60-day Game Changer seminar to change my mindset from a negative mindset to a positive one, and showed me how to monetize my passion!

Francisca Epale

My gratitude also goes to Hugh Anthony, author of *The Ultimate Guide to Public Speaking: 7 Steps to Professional Mastery* who suggested I use the words *Middle Kingdom*, instead of China, on my book cover, to make it more intriguing to readers.

My sincere appreciation to Valerie Kanay New York's CEO and Founder of Valerie Kanay Talks, Host of the Rich Flow of Life Podcast series, for mentoring me to set up a comprehensive program to accompany my book.

I am truly indebted to Rosa Greco, my personal book architect, who gave me one hundred percent guidance, support and encouragement throughout my book writing.

Dr. Nina Capo Chichi, I appreciate all the medical interpretation you did for me while I was in China.

My wonderful roommate, Shade Lapite, web design editor, I thank you for giving me some insights on writing a book.

The faculty members of the John Maxwell team: Dr. John C. Maxwell, Paul Martinelli, Ed Decosta, Melissa West, Robby Galbraith, Scott Faye, Chris Robinson and Christian Simpson. You cannot be forgotten due to all the advice, mentoring and coaching I received from the Maxwell teachings, some of which were incorporated in my book. A big thank you to Lisa Browning, the editor of the 10-10-10.com program, and

The Naked Educator

my sincere gratitude to all of those who gave me testimonials: Brian Tracey, Dr. Jim Pellegrini, Dr Lynda Davey-Longstreet, Professor Philip Alaibo, Dr. Nina Capo-Chichi and Dr. Nicoline Ambe. If I have omitted your name, please forgive me.

My sincere gratitude to Adiat Junaid, Media coach and Communications Strategist for recommending some media outlets to market my book.

My appreciation goes to Shane Madgett (former international teacher recruiter), who interviewed me via Skype from Shanghai, China. I would not have had the opportunity to teach in China and this book would not have been produced.

Finally, I would like to thank the Almighty for having spared my life when I faced a near fatal medical emergency in China.

ACCOLADES

This book is loaded with great information and good ideas that you use immediately to survive and thrive in China.

-Brian Tracy, International motivational speaker

The Naked Educator: How to Survive in the Middle Kingdom, is a must read for those planning to teach in China. As an educator myself who has been to China several times for business and education projects, and have also trained Chinese teachers in professional development programs, I can totally relate to the personal stories interwoven with humor as the culture and life-style is well-illustrated.

-Jim Pellegrini, BA.,B.Ed., M.Ed.,Ph.D., TESOL instructor,
Director of Eastern Canada Operations and International Development

This must read book, offers cogent, practical and pertinent answers to the critical questions pertaining to living in the Middle Kingdom, China, as an expatriate teacher. Francisca's compelling experiences invariably, provide a guide for every prospective English teacher or visitor to China. She passionately discusses the abundant cultural nuances, norms and practices, to enable visitors avoid mistakes, minimize risk, while optimizing the experience of visiting or living in one of the most culturally diverse countries on the face of the planet.
Professor Philip Alalibo -Faculty of General Education & Liberal Studies, Centennial College, Toronto, Canada.
Author of "A Sahara Voice: Poems from the Heart of Africa. "

Francisca Epale

A simply fascinating and captivating account of life in China from the perspective of a Canadian expatriate English teacher.
African Immigrant Magazine-Canada's Premier African Magazine

What is evident from Francisca's story is her ability to not just survive through challenging situations but to adapt to them and come out all the stronger (and wiser). Clothed in humor and honesty, Francisca's narrative is informative, and enlightening. Her story is not just for teachers thinking about their skills set by working in China, but for anyone planning to visit the middle kingdom.
Lynda Davey-Longstreet, Ph.D., B.Ed., TESL, CLB, BTC-NCLC
Settlement Counsellor and Language Assessor,
Skills for Change, Toronto, Canada

The Naked Educator sincerely catapulted me into a flash back of nostalgic experience as I sojourned in the Middle Kingdom as a medical student. I relived and emphasized with every incident in this amazing survival kit. Over my six years in China, I had toughened up my survival box but I wish I was prepared from this concise and clear book. This precious information would have helped me avoid some of the challenges I faced. I strongly recommend this book.
Dr. Nina Capo Chichi, General Practitioner
University hospital center, Brazzaville, Congo

The Naked Educator

"The Naked Educator: How to survive in the Middle Kingdom is an eye-opener about the author's intriguing journey in China. Her experience was so impactful that she wants expatriates travelling to China to be cognizant of certain aspects of the Chinese culture. The saying to be forewarned is to be forearmed applies here. The book is replete with successful character-building stories. It is a must-read.

Dr. Nicoline Ambe, Parent Education Speaker & Trainer,
Amazon #1 Bestselling author: Helping Parents Raise High Achievers.

About the Author

Francisca Epale comes from a transcultural background. Her father, the late Dr. Simon Joseph Epale (DPhil Oxford), originated from Cameroon, while her mother, the late Tessa Eunice Epale, came from Jamaica. A bilingual educator by profession, she has taught English as a second language and French at the beginner, intermediate and advanced levels. Her contributions are drawn directly from more than 20 years of teaching junior/high schools, colleges, universities and language schools in the United States of America, Canada and China. She holds a Bachelor of Arts degree in French from Edinboro University of Pennsylvania, a Master of Arts degree in teaching from Minnesota State University, and many certificates such as CTM (Competent Toastmasters), now called CC (Competent Communicator), and TESOL (Teachers of English to Speakers of Other Languages) a certificate with a specialization in Business English. Because of her interest in personal development, she is a graduate of the Landmark Forum as well as My Dreams Work, Inc. the 60-day Game Changer. For more of her credentials and accomplishments, please visit **thenakededucatorbook.com.**

Francisca is currently an accredited community French interpreter and has been selected to appear on a newsletter of MCIS (Multicultural

Francisca Epale

Community Interpreter Services) under the rubric of interpreter success stories. *The Naked Educator* is her first book; however, she has written 9 poems entitled: *Life, Work, Love, Beauty, Education, Puberty, Fear, War,* and *Death.* Additional writings include three blog posts: *The ABC'S of Toastmasters; Skills Acquired from Membership in Toastmasters,* and *A Memorable Way of Making Introductions at Networking Events.* Her master's degree thesis is on *Language Teaching Problems in a Multilingual and Multicultural Community: The Case of the Republic of Cameroon.*

Francisca has been featured in the *African Immigrant magazine* (Canada's premier African magazine), and as well as in *L'Express* (a French newspaper in Toronto as well).

As an independent certified coach, teacher and speaker with the John Maxwell Team, she is available for mastermind groups, lunch and learns, and speaking engagements. For more information, please visit **www.JohnMaxwellGroup.com/franciscaepale.** The areas she enjoys speaking about are: leadership, teaching English abroad, and personal development. Her niches are educators, women in leadership, and network marketing entrepreneurs.

The author is a member of Kingdom Speakers Toastmasters association in Toronto, Canada. Her interests include writing, personal development, aqua fit, brisk walking, and travelling.

FOREWORD

I am a big supporter of personal development. Anyone who knows me is aware that I wrote the book, *Double Your Income Doing What You Love*. In short, I help you to attain your goals in life: relationships, spiritual, emotional, financial, and professional. I met Francisca three years ago when she enrolled into my Speaker & Communication Workshop where she was a very active participant.

The Naked Educator mirrors Francisca's character-building experience in Shenzhen, China. She admits to some of her mistakes that she would not want you, as an expatriate going to the People's Republic of China, to make. The book is full of humorous anecdotes and witty expressions. Francisca shares a candid message, not only to you as an educator and graduate student in your gap year going to teach in China, but also for you to learn about another culture in a fun and easy way. *The Naked Educator: How to Survive in the Middle Kingdom* is informative, educational, entertaining and thought provoking!

Francisca is a very dedicated individual who finished her book in a very short time, as she could not hold back her eagerness to share her knowledge and expertise with you. I foresee her writing other books

Francisca Epale

in the near future and cannot wait to read them. I am truly grateful that I have been asked to foreword this book for Francisca. This book is a definite must-read!

Raymond Aaron
New York Times Bestselling Author

Chapter 1
The GENESIS

About five years ago, I had a coaching session with an executive coach/inspirational speaker, and he suggested to me that I write a book. I laughed because I could not see myself at that time as an author. Moving forward from that statement, I went to Shenzhen, China to teach English from October 2014 to October 2015. My stay was so impactful on my life that I decided to put my journey down in black and white. I did some soul-searching upon my return from southeast Asia, and vividly remembered the coach uttering these words: "You should write a book!" This statement left an indelible imprint on my mind.

This book serves as an information guide book to educators (international teacher recruiters, instructors, career coaches, principals, teachers, trainers) and college or university graduates in their gap year planning to teach in China. I do not want anyone to make the mistakes I made.

I hail from a family of writers so my heart's desire is to continue this tradition. My late father, Dr. Simon Joseph Epale, wrote six books,

Francisca Epale

while my late mother, Tessa Eunice Epale, wrote her autobiography, *Beyond the Boundaries: A Jamaican woman's triumph in Africa*, but she died before her book was completed.

It is also my desire to write a book because it is written on my bucket list and vision board.

Chapter 2
Why I Went to the Middle Kingdom

Reason for leaving Canada

Before I discuss why I went to China to teach English, I deem it necessary to provide some background information. I emigrated from the USA to Ottawa, Canada on December 1, 2001. Before immigrating to Canada, I taught beginner, intermediate and advanced French for more than 10 years in the United States of America in the public school system, community college and university.

When I came to Canada looking for a teaching job, I was told I lacked "Canadian experience," so in order to obtain the said experience, I became a member of The Capital City Toastmasters Club in Ottawa. There I obtained my CTM (Competent Toastmasters) in August 2002 which is now called CC (Competent Communicator). This certificate was obtained after having delivered ten prepared speeches, five of which I was nominated best speaker.

Now that I had acquired some "Canadian experience" with my certificate, things began looking optimistic. After I updated my resume, I applied to teach French and was invited for an interview.

Francisca Epale

The manager interviewed me entirely in the French language to test my competence in the target language. I responded confidently to each question and she said that "the French you speak in the USA is not the French that is spoken in Canada!" She also mentioned that she could not understand me despite of the fact that she asked me several questions and I responded accordingly. After an hour, the interview ended and I decided to ask the receptionist if she could understand me when I spoke French. She looked behind her back and whispered to me, "I understand your French very well; she just did not want to hire you!"

After that incident, I did my research and went to an Employment Resource Center, and was advised to apply to OCT (Ontario College of Teachers) which is the regulatory body for the teaching profession in Ontario, and is the largest self-regulatory body in Canada. The college's mandate is to license, govern and regulate the practice of teaching. My decision to teach with the TDSB (Toronto District School Board) was not possible at the time because I was declined for licensure. The reason was that I have a Bachelor of Arts degree in French and a Master of Arts degree in Education. I was informed that the requirement is that applicants should have a Bachelor's degree in Education, but I had mine in French. Also, they claimed that I was licensed in Nebraska, instead of Minnesota where I got my teacher training and my master's degree. I explained that my job offer was to teach in Nebraska, not Minnesota, so that is why I got my teaching license in Nebraska. I discussed my situation with the then MPP

The Naked Educator

(Member of Provincial Parliament) who said I could apply to become a supply teacher. A legal shield lawyer was also contacted and wrote them a letter on my behalf, but the OCT was adamant they would not license me. I even asked to take a few courses, but my request was denied. They wanted me to go back to university to obtain my Bachelors in Education in Ontario. Since I did not have my OCT license, I was unable to obtain any full time teaching jobs. To make ends meet, sometimes I would take on some non-teaching jobs. For several years I taught part time at three institutions of learning!

In order to enhance my resume, in addition to teaching French, I decided to also teach English. So, I enrolled in TESL Ontario (Teachers of English as a Second Language), and a few years later, in a TESOL course (Teachers of English to Speakers of Other Languages) with a specialization in Business English. The latter course enabled me to teach overseas. The Director of Global TESOL College, Dr. Jim Pellegrini, guaranteed me a position overseas upon completion of the course. I did my research, and when he asked every student in class where they would like to teach, I mentioned Dubai. Unfortunately, authorities in one college in Dubai said that they wanted overseas teaching experience. Then, China fell into my laps. I guess I was going to obtain the overseas experience which Dubai wanted. I recall when taking the TESOL course, the Director said, "There is a desperate need for English teachers in China. If students were to fill all the classrooms at the University of Toronto, and all of them were sent on a ship to China, there would still be a shortage of English teachers in China!"

From what has been discussed in the aforementioned paragraphs, that is how I ended up in China.

Pre-departure hiccups

The thought of travelling to China to teach scared me. I was afraid, and doubtful if I was making the right decision, because deep down in my heart I wanted to teach in Dubai in the Middle East. Going to a new country, knowing neither the language, nor the culture, gave me many sleepless nights.

My interview to China was done via Skype by an international teacher recruiter based in Shanghai, China. After working with him for a few weeks, my pre-departure hiccups began. I received a letter stating that my expected arrival date would be September 6, 2014. I then proceeded to hire a property manager who would maintain my condo while I was overseas. The first hiccup occurred when my recruiter went on medical leave, and I was assigned a younger recruiter who was new and did not know where the former recruiter had left off. She requested that I send my resume. I told her I had already sent it three times. She said, "Send it again." The situation was that my resume was not a Chinese-style resume. I politely asked her to send me a sample of a Chinese-style resume, which she later did, and I copied the sample. That was my second hiccup.

Renting my condo

The third incident which did not go well was that, because I was informed my expected arrival date would be September 6 2014, I rented my condo for September 1, 2014, through a property management company. The new recruiter was unable to process all the documents on time, because, at one time, my signed contract landed in the first recruiter's junk e-mail, and he did not know it was there until a week later! My arrival date changed from September 6, 2014 to October 22, 2014. I was livid because I had no place to live from August 31 to October 22, 2014!!

When I shared my dilemma with my new recruiter, she casually said, "Oh, this gives you more time to spend some personal time with your friends." I told her that I did not have a place to live because I had already rented out my condo. She discussed my situation with her supervisor but they were adamant that the date could not be changed to an earlier one. Here I was, calling around Toronto like a fool, looking for a place to stay. I could not afford to stay at a hotel for seven weeks; that would have been very expensive. Luckily, I found two people to stay with. I stayed with one for four weeks, and with the other for three weeks.

Francisca Epale

My belongings

The fourth hiccup I faced was what to do with my belongings. Should I sell them or put them in storage? I decided to sell my things and give the rest away to charity because putting things in storage would be expensive for one year, which was the duration I initially planned to stay in China. The fifth situation I faced was to decide which city in China to choose to live in. I was asked by the recruiter to choose either Beijing, Shanghai or Shenzhen. I decided to choose the last mentioned city because of the weather, the population, and the fact that it was adjacent to Hong Kong, where many people speak English.

Finally, after all the pre-departure hiccups ended, I was airborne on Cathay Pacific, in Premium Economy, to Shenzhen, China via Hong Kong. It was a bitter-sweet experience for me. To crown all, I was assured that someone would pick me up at Shenzhen airport to take me to my hotel, where I would live temporarily for two weeks.

The Middle Kingdom

China is one of the oldest cultures in the entire world, with a rich history that dates back for thousands of years. Throughout the last 5000 years, China has been known by many different names, but, the most traditional name that China has been known by, is Zhonghou, which means Middle Kingdom (or, sometimes translated as, Central kingdom).

Ethnocentrism, the belief that one's own country is the center of the world in a cultural or historical standpoint, is not extremely uncommon. Citizens of the United States, for example, refer to themselves as Americans, even though there are over 30 other countries in North and South America.

There is a particular significance to China calling themselves the center, or middle, of the world. The term has evolved to mean different things over the years, from a geographical and political perspective; but, why is China called the Middle kingdom, exactly? Thousands of years ago, China was divided into multiple independent states before it was unified by an emperor. During this period, the term Middle Kingdom, or Central State, was used to refer to the actual middle areas of these states. The term reflected the culturally significant regions of China that were located along the valley of the Yellow river.

In later years, after China became more of a unified empire, Middle Kingdom referred to the region in which the emperor lived. This ultimately meant that the Middle Kingdom was actually a dynamic, shifting region, depending on the period of history you look at, and which emperor was ruling. As the time passed, the term Middle Kingdom referred to the entire country as a whole, instead of a small area within China itself. In the 19th and 20th centuries, the term Middle Kingdom shifted to mean the country as a whole, instead of describing individual states, in an attempt to give solidarity to the

Chinese people. By referring to their country as the Middle Kingdom, the people of China imply their significance in the world, and use the term as a form of pride to be a collective and single nation. Ultimately, the answer to the question of why China is called the Middle Kingdom, is an answer that shifts throughout history, from referring to a small collective region, to eventually encompassing the nation and its people as a whole. Now that I have discussed why I went to the Middle Kingdom, chapter three will be about the language and culture.

Chapter 3
Language and Culture

56 ethnic groups

Chinese culture is one of the world's oldest cultures, dating thousands of years old. The area in which the culture is dominant covers a large geographical region in eastern Asia, with customs and traditions varying greatly between provinces, cities, and even towns as well. There are 56 officially recognized ethnic groups in China. Han Chinese is by far the largest group. Throughout History, many groups have merged into neighboring ethnicities, or disappeared. At the same time, many within the Han identity have maintained distinct linguistic and regional traditions. The term Zhonghua Minzu has been used to describe the notion of Chinese nationalism in general. Much of the traditional identity within the community has to do with distinguishing the family name (Wikipedia).

Male expatriates and Chinese women relationships

While I was in China, I noticed that three quarters of the male expatriate teachers had either a Chinese wife or girlfriend. I understood that Chinese women literally run after foreign men, and the former are easy prey! One day, just out of curiosity, I asked five Chinese female students randomly why they love foreign men so much. They all said, "Foreign men are more romantic, and they do it well!"

Since there are many Chinese/foreigner relationships, it is important to know something about their legal system. We were interviewed by the police when some teachers and I went to get our permanent resident visas in the police station. One of the issues the police brought up is that if there were a dispute between a Chinese and an expatriate, which might lead to a law suit, priority and favoritism will be given to the Chinese person.

Two favorite topics for conversation

One aspect of Chinese culture I found very interesting were two favorite topics of conversation: food and family. "Have you ever been shocked to sit next to your Chinese friends and realized where does all this noise come from? Yet all of a sudden, you realize that it is YOUR Chinese friend next to you chewing like a cow? Oh God, how embarrassing is that? Eating and fulfilling and satisfying hunger has long been a very important aspect in Chinese culture. To show appreciation and the delicate cuisine we present it by making chewing noise to show it. Even when drinking hot tea for instance, the louder the noise we make, the more it indicates the savor of such tea. When you as a foreigner spotted such an act from your Chinese friends

/employees/relationship partners, it would be lovely to give some tolerance of hiding it in your thought and blaming for such bad manners. A little bit of nudge quickly to him /her would be highly appreciated." –*Why Do Chinese People Eat With Their Mouth Open?* The Cultural Frontier, April 4, 2013.

Some interesting facts about food culture in China are as follows:
1-Do not roll rice into a ball.
2- Do not spread out rice to cool.
3-Do not crunch bones with your teeth.
4-Do not grab what you want.
5-Do not replace meat and fish that you have already tasted.
6-Do not stir or add condiments.
7- Do not throw bones to the dogs.
8- Do not pick your teeth.
(*Food Culture in China* by Jacqueline M. Newman)

"Those whose behavior, at the table or elsewhere, is less than proper, are called foreign devils. The Chinese believe that non-Chinese do not know the rules, and, therefore eat differently. They do not want to be such devils. People who eat impolitely are considered foreign because the Chinese know not a manner deemed rude or impolite. Therefore, each Chinese person takes a first bite of food when correct to do so, and not before an elder and/or guest."

"There are things that the Chinese rush to do at the table. These include rushing to give someone special items from the service dishes before helping themselves. Another important behavior is, when appropriate and polite, to take food from the closest side from the common platter or bowl. Getting up and reaching is considered rude. Stretching or standing to get something for oneself is absolutely forbidden. It is preferred that only the host stands to acquire a special tidbit, and then to give that to an elder or honored guest. There are several other polite or impolite things different from in western culture. It is polite, and considered acceptable, to make slurping sounds when consuming soup. That is deemed acceptable because making noise sucks in air, cools the soup, and avoids burning the mouth. In addition, slurping indicates that the item is liked. It is impolite to stand chop sticks upright in food. That action is interpreted as wishing someone dead. Another rule is to never lick chop sticks, a behavior that is also considered exceptionally rude. There are other dos and don'ts; they can be found in any Chinese book of etiquette, and they can also be seen and practiced when following the behaviors of others at meal time."
(*Food Culture in China* by Jacqueline M. Newman)

Apart from food, the next topic Chinese nationals like discussing, is family. They enjoy discussions concerning family, so it is not uncommon for Chinese learners to ask their foreign teachers the following question: Teacher, do you live alone? They are indirectly asking if you have a partner. They also tend to ask other personal

questions such as
- How old are you?
- Do you have children?
- What do you do on your days off?
- Do you cook?
- How much money do you earn?
- How much is your rent?
- How long do you plan to stay in China?
- Do you like Chinese food?
- Do you like China?

When discussing the culture of China, one cannot omit their holidays and festivals. "Chinese culture has a history of some five thousand years. During this time, a great variety of unique, traditional festivals have evolved. Chinese festivals are rooted deeply in popular tradition, and despite China's many changes they remain firmly established as part of its colorful culture."

"Most of the festivals in ancient China were connected with the development of astronomy, the calendar and mathematics. Many developed from what became twenty-four seasonal division points under the traditional Chinese lunar calendar, all of which have been more or less established by the time of the Han Dynasty (206 BC-AD 220)." (*Chinese Festivals* by Liming Wei)

Holidays and festivals

The following are a list of popular festivals in China:

Traditional Festivals
1- Laba festival
2- Spring festival
3- Yuanxiao festival
4- Spring Dragon festival
5- Pure Brightness festival
6- Dragon Boat festival
7- Ullam-bana festival
8- Mid-Autumn festival
9- Double Ninth festival

Statutory Festivals
1- New Year's day
2- Women's day
3- Tree-planting day
4- International Labour day
5- Youth day
6- International Children's day
7- Army day
8- Teacher's day
9- National day
10- Chinese New Year

(Chinese Festivals by Liming Wei)

The Naked Educator

I deem it necessary to describe one of the holidays which is very important in Chinese culture. The Chinese New Year is a holiday that celebrates the importance of family and friends. Preparing for the new year and a new start in life is just as important as celebrating the first day of the New Year and the parades that follow. You can do many things to enjoy the New Year:

Make banners with good-luck wishes and poems on them.
Give them to your teachers, neighbors, and friends.
Visit your grandparents, aunts and uncles.
Take them a lucky banner you have made.
Take flowers or fruits to family members and friends.
Clean your room and help clean the house.

The Chinese New Year is based on the Chinese calendar. It is different from the calendar used in the United States. Each year of the Chinese calendar is named after one of the twelve animals. The animals are: the rat, the ox, the tiger, the rabbit, the dragon, the snake, the horse, the sheep (or goat), the monkey, the rooster, the dog, and the pig. After twelve years, the animals repeat in the same order again.

The Chinese believe you share some traits with the animal that rules the year in which you were born. The rat is friendly and busy. The ox is loyal and dependable. The tiger is brave and quick to act. The rabbit is shy and quiet. The dragon is strong and wise. The snake is tricky and cautious. The horse is cheerful and free-spirited. The sheep is trustworthy and lonely. The monkey is funny and mischievous. The rooster is proud and hardworking. The dog is loyal and faithful. The pig is smart and kind. A dragon has special meaning for the Chinese. It stands for strength and good luck. Every Chinese New Year parade ends with a dragon made of bamboo poles and paper or silk. The Chinese dragon is strong because it is made up of the parts of many animals. It has the eyes of a rabbit, the mouth of a camel, the claws of a hawk, the legs of a tiger, the ears of an ox, and the body of a snake (Chinese New Year by Alice K. Flanagan, Svetlana Zurikina, Linda Labbo). Now that language and culture has been discussed, the next chapter is about teaching in the Middle Kingdom.

Chapter 4
Teaching in the Middle Kingdom

I had the privilege of teaching at an international education company which specializes in language training, in Shenzhen, with a population of 10,778,900 (2014) [Wikipedia]. The city has a very mild winter and it was extremely hot. Shenzhen is located north of Hong Kong so this gave me an outlet to visit Hong Kong at least once a month on my days off. The company has branches located all around the world, and, while I was in China, it celebrated its 50th anniversary.

White-collar professionals

The clients I taught were mostly white-collar professionals: engineers, medical doctors, computer analysts. There were also a few housewives as well. Some of the students had the opportunity to be sponsored by their company to learn English for six months. These learners were on the most part very serious about studying English. Fortunately, the school where I taught also hired Chinese teachers who taught English. These teachers majored in English at university and have been speaking English since they were in kindergarten. The Chinese teachers usually taught beginner and elementary classes, while the expatriate teachers would normally teach intermediate and advanced classes, or a blend of both lower and higher levels, depending on the population of the center. Having discussed the kind of clients who attended this school, I will discuss the kind of class room settings.

Types of classes

There were four kinds of classes students could choose from: 1- Face to face, 2- Workshops, 3-Life Clubs, and, 4- Career Advancement Events. Face to face classes consisted of a minimum of one client and a maximum of four clients. Face to face teaching were for clients who were shy, or wanted more individualized attention, and they paid a higher tuition than for the other classes. Face to face classes were held in small classrooms to accommodate the smaller number of clients.

In addition to teaching face to face classroom style, I also facilitated workshops which could hold a maximum of twenty eight students. One advantage of these workshops was that there was more interaction, activities, games, and less teacher- talk time. Another kind of teaching was that of the life clubs. This was my favorite, for they were similar to conversation circles. The teachers had to choose a theme and teach anything associated with it. For example, I chose travel, and taught concepts like French-speaking countries, their capitals and their flags, in the form of a game. Dream vacations came up as one of the concepts taught. Also under the rubric of travel, I taught how to travel to Shenzhen, Guangzhou and Hong Kong, using the subway. The clients also learnt how to read airline, train and bus tickets. Another topic under travel was the case study of Jordan Alexis and Elizabeth Gallagher, who travelled around the world together. Jordan had bought airline tickets for himself and his girlfriend Elizabeth Gallagher, but the girl friend broke up with him before the major trip. He did not want the ticket to go to waste because it was non-refundable, so he went on a social media site to find a lady holder of a Canadian passport, with the same name, who would accompany him on the trip around the world on December 21, 2014. I asked the students if something like that could happen in China. The students were divided fifty-fifty. The next kind of class taught was career advancement. I found this course easy to teach because I had attended many job search and related workshops in Ottawa and Toronto, Canada. Having discussed the four types of classes we taught, I will now discuss the levels of student competencies.

Levels of Student Competencies

There are fourteen levels, and to be promoted to the next level at my center, each client had to take an oral placement test.

	Levels	Stages
1	OA, OB1	Beginner
2	2,3,4	Elementary
3	5,6,7	Intermediate
4	8,9,10	Upper intermediate
5	11,12,13	Advanced
6	14	Upper advanced

Each level came with its joys and sorrows, but my favorite levels to teach were intermediate and above, because the clients could speak English fairly fluently. We cannot talk about levels of student competencies without mentioning the teaching styles.

Teaching Styles

The teaching style I used was the Cartesian principle, where I reduced everything to the simplest. I used both inductive and deductive approaches. An inductive approach to teaching language starts with examples and asks learners to find the rules. For example, if I am teaching beginner students the plural, I will teach it as follows:

Singular	Plural
pen	pens
teacher	teachers
book	books

I will then ask the students looking at the board how we form the plural. This is a student-centered approach with less teacher-talk time. "On the other hand the deductive approach to teaching language starts by giving learners rules, then examples, then practice. The deductive approach may be suitable with lower levels learners who need a clear base from which to begin with a new language item, or with learners who are accustomed to a more traditional approach, and so who lack the training to find rules themselves. (*Teaching English*, British Council)

Other teaching styles included observation, paired activities, group activities, and repetition using class, groups, men, women, and individuals. I tailored my teaching styles to the levels of the students, their gender and occupations. For example, if I were teaching a class full of engineers, I could discuss scientific concepts for better understanding and enjoyment of the class. On the other hand, if I were teaching a face to face class with four housewives, I would tailor the lesson and include examples of children and house chores. After talking about teaching styles, I deem it necessary to talk about types of learners, for teaching and learning styles are mutually exclusive.

Learning styles

There are four primary learning styles: visual, auditory, read-write and kinesthetic. People learn using a variety of these methods, but one method is usually predominant. Familiarity with the characteristics of each learning style, and associated strategies, allows you to address the needs of each type of learner.

Visual learners

Visual learners are characterized by the following:
- They tend to be fast talkers
- They exhibit impatience and have a tendency to interrupt
- They use words and phrases that evoke visual images
- They learn by seeing and visualizing

The teaching style for visual learners should include the use of demonstrations and visually pleasing materials, and you should make an effort to paint mental pictures for your learners.

Auditory learners

Auditory learners are characterized by the following:

- They speak slowly and tend to be natural listeners
- They think in a linear manner
- They prefer to have things explained to them verbally rather than to read written information
- They learn by listening and verbalizing.

The teaching strategy for auditory learners should sound good and should be planned and delivered in the form of an organized conversation.

Read-write learners

Read-write learners are characterized by the following:

- They prefer information to be displayed in writing, such as lists of ideas.
- They emphasize text-based input and output
- They enjoy reading and writing in all forms.

Your teaching methods for read-write learners should include writing out keys words in list form. The students will learn by silently reading or rewriting their notes repeatedly; writing out in their own words the ideas and principles that were taught or discussed; organizing any diagrams, graphs, other visual depictions into statements (for example, "The trend is . . ."), and putting reactions, actions, diagrams, charts and flowcharts into words. They like multiple-choice tests.

Kinesthetic learners

Kinesthetic learners are characterized by the following:

- They tend to be the slowest talkers of all
- They tend to be slow to make decisions
- They use all their senses to engage in learning
- They learn by doing and solving real-life problems.

- They like hands-on approaches to things and learn through trial and error.

The teaching style for kinesthetic learners should include hands-on demonstrations and case examples to be discussed and solved.

There are a variety of types of learners in a single classroom. Therefore it is important to incorporate multiple teaching methods.
(*How to Teach Effectively* – Lyceum Books, Inc.)

Career advancement events

Career advancement events were geared to intermediate and advanced level students. I thoroughly enjoyed facilitating these events because, even though there was a syllabus, the instructors could always add their own twist to it. The syllabi consisted of different teachers who wrote each lesson and made it available for others to use on a database. An example of a typical lesson was the Myers Briggs personality tests. For more information on the Myers Briggs please visit my website at **thenakededucatorbook.com**. While teaching in China, I formed a habit of giving examples in the western world, as well as the eastern world, so that the students could relate to any discussion. For example, when facilitating career advancement events, I mentioned a millionaire blogger, Tracey Walker, whom I met on the internet and later connected with, via Skype, to listen to her webinar. I would then ask for a similar example in China. I shared with my students the 21 day blogging challenge to help them with goal-setting and accountability:

1- What is your monthly income goal for 2015?
2- Who is the number one person you would like to meet?
3- If you had all the money you ever needed, what would you do with your life?
4- What is the number one thing you are going to do different this year?
5- How many times a year do you want to take your family on vacation?
6- What has been your greatest achievement?
7- Why does your success matter?
8- What is your favorite book of all time?
9- What is the number one piece of advice you would give to someone starting their own business?
10- What is your dream car?
11- What made you become an entrepreneur?
12- If you were to move to another city, where would it be?
13- Who influenced you the most in 2014?
14- What is the number one thing you can do to be healthier?
15- What is the number one place you want to travel to this year?
16- What is your favorite season and why?
17- What is the next thing you want to accomplish?
18- How will having a successful business change your life?
19- What do you want your legacy to be?

20- Who are you targeting your message to this year?
21- How has the 21-day challenge helped you?
(Tracey Walker - Millionaire Blogger)

I recall a lesson I taught, in the career advancement course, that was SWOT (strengths, weaknesses, opportunities, and threats analysis).

	Positive	Negative
Internal	Strengths	Weaknesses
External	Opportunities	Threats

I divided the SWOT into graphs for the visual learner. Everyone who wants to succeed in business and in life should be familiar with SWOT analysis. Another aspect of the course which I included was some personal development such as Jack Canfield's 30-day guide to living the Law of Attraction which is as follows:

1- Vision word
2- Like attracts like
3- Like energy
4- You are a magnet
5- Thoughts are things
6- Your mind
7- Emotions
8- Importance of Joy
9- Forgiveness

10- Focus on the positive
11- Abundance
12- Expansion
13- Life Purpose
14- Live on Purpose
15- What do you want
16- One outrageous goal
17- Repetition
18- Affirmations
19- Specific Affirmations
20- Visualization
21- Alternative method
22- Your vision book
23- How to use your vision book
24- Attitude
25- Negative people
26- Higher power
27- Daily meditation
28- Taking action
29- Daily rituals
30- Believing

For more information on the 30-day guide to living the law of attraction kindly visit **thenakededucatorbook.com**

This lesson was a great success; after class one of my students asked, "Teacher, have you read the book, *The Secret*, by Rhonda Byrne?" I told her it is also a movie, but I have not read it. She urged me to buy the book, so I asked her if she had read it in English or Chinese. She laughed, and said, "In Chinese." I asked her where I could get the English version, and she blurted out, "Hong Kong." It was my day off the next day so I made a special trip to Hong Kong to buy the book, "The Secret", and I finished reading it in two days, and I thoroughly enjoyed it. The student came up to me and asked, "Teacher, did you go to Hong Kong and buy the book?" I responded affirmatively.

Lounge chats

At least twice a week, the teachers in my center were required to sit down with students on the sofas and talk about anything of interest to the students. Fei (her name has been changed to protect the privacy of the student) happened to be one of the students in our lounge chats. She blurted out excitedly, "Let's talk about the book, The Secret." I told her to impart to the other students what the book was about, and any takeaways. It was a good thing I had just read the book so that I could relate to what Fei was saying. I then asked the other students for any stories of visualizations that they could share with the person sitting next to them. I then shared a story of visualization I had read in a book, and they all listened attentively. There was a young man who came from a very impoverished family and his dream was to become a medical doctor. He could not afford to go to medical school, so he came up with a brilliant idea and decided to volunteer to clean a doctor's office. The doctor accepted, and the next day the young man came in very early, cleaned the office, and stood in front of the doctor's diplomas and began visualizing his name on the diplomas. He was so focused that when the doctor came in he did not hear him. The doctor cleared his throat, and the young man was startled. Dr. K asked him, "Excuse me, what were you doing?" The man answered, "My dream is to become a medical doctor. I do not have the means to go to medical school, so I was just visualizing my name on your diplomas."

Dr. K empathized with him and asked him to sit down, and the former asked the latter, "Tell me, on a scale of one to ten, one being the lowest, and ten the highest score, how badly do you want to go to medical school?" The volunteer janitor said, "Ten," and tears literally ran down his face. Dr. K told him to dry his eyes and go home. That evening, Dr. K shared the incident with his wife. She suggested to him, "Why don't we pay for him to go to medical school?" That is how the fellow, who had no means of going to medical school, had someone volunteer to help him out. I told my students, during lounge chats, that the power of visualization is very important.

Many times, during lounge chats, I would tell them to ask me any questions. One client asked, "Is it true that everyone in America has a gun?" I laughed, and said, "No, everyone does not carry a gun." I lived in the United States for seventeen years before immigrating to Canada, and I neither held nor owned a gun. There are more than three hundred million people in the United States, so that would be a lot of guns to possess! Then I turned the question back and asked what happens in China. They said the firearm ownership law in the Peoples' Republic of China heavily regulates the ownership of firearms. Generally, private citizens are not allowed to possess firearms. Another student said, "I hear westerners sleep around." Then I laughed again. "It is really impossible for all westerners to sleep around. Some do, but not all." Then I asked, "What about China?" They said things have changed a lot in China due to western influence. Some Chinese live together without being married, and some women get pregnant without being married. I then said jokingly, "Would you call that sleeping around?" All the students laughed, and I told them to avoid stereotypes and generalizations because they can impede their progress in life. The good thing about the lounge chats was that I learnt about some Chinese culture, while they learnt about western culture.

From my recollection of teaching in China, one of the major differences between teaching in other countries such as Canada, the United States, Australia, the United Kingdom, and Ireland, is that teachers should try to speak a little slower, and pronounce the words more audibly.

Do not put this book down yet! Wait until you read the next chapter!

Chapter 5
SUCCESS STORIES

Event planner for 60 instructors

My stay in China was bitter-sweet, and nothing is more fascinating than to share some success stories. The first success story I am proud to share is when I was asked to coordinate two events for teachers so that they could get to know each other, and to break the monotony of teaching. I was given 2000 RMB to host an event. The first event was eating in a Thai restaurant, which I co-coordinated with a Chinese teacher. The other was eating in an American restaurant at SeaWorld which I coordinated entirely alone. The teachers liked the second restaurant better because it was in Shekou, a high-end, expensive place which is mostly inhabited by expatriates. For the second restaurant, because the teachers enjoyed the food so much, the coordinator supervisor added some extra money to the budget. I was given a chance to use my event planning skills. I chose eating in a restaurant because, as I had indicated earlier, the two favorite topics for Chinese are family and food. Sometimes other instructors planned events such as horse-back riding, mountain climbing, pedicures, manicures, yoga and painting. These events were open to all teachers, especially the new teachers. This gave us an opportunity of meeting teachers from other centers. These events were free for the teachers, and they were sponsored by the school. One teacher thought of the idea of having events for teachers to attend, and a budget was allocated for thirty instructors. If a restaurant was chosen, we always made sure to choose different kinds of cuisine such as American, Indian, Mexican, German, and Japanese, as well as other nationalities.

Support group for expatriates

I joined a support group for expatriates on WeChat, which is a popular Chinese instant message site. On WeChat, if I needed anything such as a good dry cleaner, I would text my information and someone would respond. If I wanted to have lunch or dinner with someone on my day off, I could invite someone on the site. Expatriates tended to be close to each other since we were in a foreign country. Sometimes, when we met other expatriates on the street, we stopped and had a small chat; many times we exchanged contact information. One of the expatriates, who is married to a German, organized monthly events, where, on the first Saturday of the month, we would meet at a restaurant and eat. At the first event, there were twenty eight ladies, and the server said he has never served so many foreign ladies in one seating. Another hot topic in this support group was about finding a good hairstylist. I discovered one out of town for ethnic hair, so I became the go-to person when any one wanted their hair done.

Submission of lessons for career advancement events

At each center where I taught, one teacher was assigned to facilitate Career Advancement Events. If the center was a big one, then two teachers were assigned. After three months, I was transferred to another center to teach because one teacher quit abruptly, and they needed a replacement as soon as possible. There were monthly mandatory meetings for career advancement events, and during the month we had to submit as many lessons as we could for a prize and recognition at our monthly meetings. For the short time I held this role, I submitted two lessons for them to add to their database. During this time, I did not see myself being in China for long, so my plan B was to enroll in an online course to be certified as a John Maxwell teacher, speaker and coach. It was easy for me to come up with a lesson, combining my personal development seminars and workshops I had attended in the past in Canada.

Alternate medicine

One of the most powerful success stories happened when I had a medical emergency and I was asked to have surgery. I had the good fortune of working with four highly qualified doctors: my family doctor, Dr. Su; traditional Chinese medicine, Dr. Wong; acupuncturist, Dr. Zhou; obstetrician /gynecologist, Dr. Qin; as well as Dr. Nina Capo Chichi, who served as interpreter for Dr. Qin. After asking several questions, I decided that if I were to have surgery, I would do it in

Canada. Using acupuncture and traditional Chinese medicine were eye-openers for me. Acupuncture is a system of complementary medicine that involves pricking the skin or tissues with needles; it is used to alleviate pain and to treat various physical, mental and emotional conditions. Originating in ancient China, acupuncture is now widely practiced in the west. The possible benefits of acupuncture are:

1- When performed correctly, it is safe.
2- There are very few side effects.
3- It is a very effective combination treatment.
4- It may be considered for patients who do not respond to pain medications.
5- It is a useful alternative for patients who do not want to take pain medication.

(medicalnewstoday.com/articles)

Acupuncture is a component of the health care system of China that can be traced back at least 2,500 years ago. The general theory of acupuncture is based on the premise that there are patterns of energy flowing through the body that are essential for health. Disruptions of this flow are believed to be responsible for disease.

Traditional Chinese medicine, popularly known as TCM, is a style of Asian medicine informed by modern medicine but built on the foundation of more than 2,500 years of medical practice that includes various forms of herbal medicine, acupuncture, massage, exercise and dietary therapy. It is primarily used as a complimentary alternative medicine approach:

1- All natural: The medicine is all natural. Although the herbs that are used in the medicine may have some side effects, it is nothing compared to the side effects from modern medicine.
2- The source: With traditional Chinese medicine, they had more of a goal of finding what was causing illness and healing it. They did not choose to focus on healing the symptoms. Modern medicine tends to just treat the symptoms.
3- Range: TCM has been known to treat a broad range of things. It is able to treat things from headaches and PMS, to things like helping to treat addictions and the common flu.
4- Improve general health: It is able to improve a person's health overall. This is because it does not rely on things such as modern drugs. Because of this, you do not get all the side effects that would normally occur, such as drowsiness from the medication.
5- Balance: TCM has started to become favored because it does not just focus on the physical part of being ill. It works on returning the mind, the body and the soul, to proper balance.
6- Focused: With this type of medicine, it is more focused on trying to find a diagnosis. An example of this is when someone has a cold, they try to figure out exactly what type of cold it is.
7- Potency: A good thing about this kind of medicine is the potency of the cures.

8- Treatments: Unlike modern medicine, the Chinese medicine offers a broader range of treatments. With modern medicine the main thing is usually to get prescribed some medication, but with TCM there are things like herbs, massages and food therapies, among other things.
9- Side effects: With this form of medicine, with herbs, there are very few side effects. Unlike modern medication, where some of the side effects can be very dire, most of the effects that come with herbs, for the most part, are harmless.
10- Multiple uses: With TCM there are usually multiple uses such as calming anxiety or helping with sleep, or even being a tonic for things like blood and nerves.

My acupuncturist appointments at the hospital were three times a week for a duration of three months. Someone teased me that, due to going to the hospital so frequently, I should have made friends with all the nurses and doctors! For the TCM (traditional Chinese Medicine) I was scheduled by the doctor to drink it twice a day for ninety days. The herbs were the bitterest drink I had ever drunk in my entire life!!! I told my doctor and he suggested I stir in some honey, but it was still very bitter. I opted for the traditional Chinese medicine instead of surgery in China because I was supposed to recuperate at home for three months. After using acupuncture and the traditional Chinese medicine, I lost ten pounds, which was good for my overall health. I spent 10,000 RMB ($2000 Canadian) on medication. I asked someone at my center where to locate the claim forms so that I could send it to my insurance to be reimbursed. He said to me, "Do not waste your time. You will get hardly anything back." I learnt through my personal development: "Do not let anyone's criticism or judgment define who you are" (Les Brown, Motivational speaker). I ignored him and filed my claims with all my original receipts. About three weeks later, the insurance company emailed me and said I began my treatment in November, but my new coverage starts in January, and does not cover Traditional Chinese medicine, so it would not be covered. I did not respond, but prayed over the situation because 10,000 RMB is a lot of money for Chinese standards. A week later, I received a phone call from the insurance company saying that they had made a mistake and that they would cover my claim, but one receipt I mailed did not have the hospital stamp on it. I asked for the amount which did not have a hospital stamp. The agent said 10 Yuan, the equivalent of two Canadian dollars! I told the agent that the cost to mail it back, and for me to go back to the hospital and have it stamped, and take the train back and forth and mail it back, would be more than 10 Yuan! He said that it is Chinese law and he would not want to be audited. I asked to speak to his supervisor and he said they would email me back. I received another email two days later saying that everything was okay, and I would receive a reimbursement of 5000 RMB; that was 50% of what it had cost . This was a success story for me because initially they did not want to cover it, but then I got some extra money.

Francisca Epale

Hired as a private French tutor

I was introduced to a Chinese family who were looking for a private French tutor for their seven year old son. This was like manna from heaven for me. His former French tutor was preparing for her final examinations and she wanted to devote more time to her studies. Also she was about to graduate and leave China. She asked if I could take over her position and I responded positively. I taught this young boy for three months but had to stop because the family was travelling to France for summer vacation. This was a success story for me because, not only did I get some money back from my insurance, I was making some extra money through private French tutoring, something I never dreamt I would be doing in China. This boy was an only child and the parents were very strict with him. They made sure he applied himself assiduously. As I was teaching the son, the father would drop by for about ten minutes to see how he was doing. The father said he enjoyed my method of teaching and was pleased with my credentials before I started teaching his son.

Visited Guangzhou and Hong Kong

Before coming to China, I was already in touch with a teacher who was living and teaching in Guangzhou. "It is known historically as Canton, and nicknamed the city of flowers. Guangzhou is the capital of Guangdong province in South China. It is the third largest city, after Beijing and Shanghai." [Wikipedia]. I discovered that this city had many black people who live and work there. The nickname for Guangzhou is "chocolate city", or "little Africa", as has been dubbed by the Chinese press. She said that there are many hairdressers for black women. When I arrived in Shenzhen, the city I chose to teach in, I went to several hairdressers and they told me they do not do ethnic hair, and that I needed to go to Guangzhou. I asked many expatriates I met at our Bible study and WeChat groups, and everyone directed me to Guangzhou. I had no choice but to go there to have my hair done, so I arranged with the teacher there to take me to get my hair done. I went by train, and to get to Guangzhou rail way station, it took about two hours, than another forty minutes to get to the hairdresser. To crown all, it took about three hours to get to a hairdresser who could do my hair!

She took me to a mall to get my hair done. A lady was standing in the hallway and she asked me, "Do you want to have your hair done?" I told her I did, and I noticed she had some difficulties communicating in English, so I asked her if she was French-speaking. She agreed so I switched and started speaking to her in French. After she finished my hair, I took a tour of the mall and I noticed a Nigerian restaurant! I usually went to Guangzhou for two things: first to do my hair, and second to eat some good African food at the Nigerian restaurant.

Apart from visiting Guangzhou, I was adventurous enough to travel to Hong Kong by myself. "Hong Kong is a city, and former British colony, in southeastern China. Vibrant and densely populated, it's a major port and global financial center famed for its tower-studded skyline. It is also known for its lively food scene – from Cantonese dim sum to extravagant high tea – and its shopping." [Facts about Hong Kong]. I needed a visa to enter Hong Kong, and each time I visited Hong Kong, I was eligible for a three-month visa! I liked Hong Kong so much that I went at least every two months. Fortunately, for me, I have visited places like The Big Buddha, (a Chinese God), which is a large bronze statue completed in 1993 and located in Ngong Ping, Lantau Island, in Hong Kong. The Big Buddha has become a major landmark in Hong Kong, attracting numerous local and overseas Buddhists and visitors. It is a valuable heritage of mankind. While at Landau island, I had the rare opportunity of riding in a cable car, which is on my bucket list as one of the things I will do before I leave this world! Another site I visited with a friend was the Avenue of Stars. It is modeled after the Hollywood's Walk of Fame, and located along the Victoria Harbour waterfront in Tsim Tsha Tsui. Another popular sight that I had the opportunity to visit was Ladies Market, on Tong Choi Street. When visiting Ladies Market, there were a lot of different things to do, depending on your interests and how much time you have, but do consider some window shopping, enjoying the atmosphere of the district, stocking up on gifts for yourself and family, eating some of the local foods, and visiting some of the nearby attractions. Ladies Market is a must-visit location for fashion lovers with an eye for bargain-priced clothing, bags, accessories, cosmetics and household products.

Coaching a student on job offers

I will now segue in talking about how I coached one of my students in making an important decision. I enrolled in July 2015 to become certified as a John Maxwell, teacher, trainer, coach and speaker, so I used some of what I had learned to apply myself assiduously in helping the student. Jane Doe (her name has been changed to protect the identity of the student) said to me:

Jane : Teacher Francisca, can you help me please?
Francisca: Yes, how can I help you?
Jane: I have two job offers and would like you to tell me which one to take.
Francisca: Two job offers!   You are a very lucky person. Congratulations. Would you like to have lunch with me downstairs, and while we wait for the server to bring our food, we can discuss your options?
Jane: Good idea.
Francisca: Jane, I will ask you a series of questions so that you can arrive at a more informed decision.
Jane: Okay.
Francisca: First of all, Jane, what made you decide to ask me, and not any other teacher in the center?
Jane: Well, teacher, you are the only one who talks about having a positive mindset, visualization, reciting daily positive affirmations and personal development.

Francisca Epale

Francisca: I see. Jane, on the back of your exercise book I would like you to draw a big letter T, and I will ask you further questions:

1- What are the names of the companies? Write each answer under the left side for the first company and under the right side for the other company.
2- What is the mission statement of each company?
3- What are the hours of operation?
4- Are they full time or part time?
5- When are your start dates?
6- Which company resonates with you from a scale of 1- 10?
7- Where is each company located in proximity to your home or school?
8- What is the reputation of each company?
9- Which company requires knowledge of English?
10- List some names of family members who can help you with your decision.
11- What are the job duties and the kind of training provided?

Jane: This information is helpful, so, if you were me, which company would you choose?

Francisca: Jane, I am not in a position to tell you which job to choose. All I can do is guide you to make your own decision.
Jane: Teacher, if you tell me which job to choose, what would happen?
Francisca: There might be consequences. For example, if I tell you which job to choose, and a month later the job does not work out,

you will blame me! Please ask the opinion of the Operations Manager.

Jane and I went back upstairs, and she asked the Operations Manager, who said, "You will have to make the decision by yourself." I then asked her to discuss it with her counselor. Jane admitted that the counselor told her the same thing. Finally, after two days when I came back from my weekend, Jane took to my coaching and chose the job herself. I felt that was one of my successful stories. Coaching Jane was out of my own volition, and I am happy she finally decided on her own to choose which company to work for.

Having shared my success stories, the next chapter deals with something more exciting: how living in China made me a stronger individual, personally, professionally and spiritually. It built my character for the better.

Chapter 6
Character Building Experiences

Apartment hunting

When I arrived in Shenzhen, on October 22, 2014, the new expatriate instructors were lodged at the Holiday Inn Express for two weeks. While lodging at this hotel, a housing agent helped us find suitable accommodation. The first apartment she showed me was very old, dirty and dilapidated. We were already warned that the first few apartments would be sub-standard, but I never imagined them to be that bad! I got upset and asked her, "If I were the housing agent, and you were the future tenant, would you live in an apartment like this?" She answered, "I already have my own place." I said, "I understand, but pretend as if you were looking for a place to live. Would you choose to live here?" She said, "We Chinese people can live anywhere." I told her politely that I could not live in a cockroach-infested apartment. It was my first week in China, and I was already building up my character. The agent showed me six apartments until I found one which was brand new, so I decided to take it in order to be the first occupant, and the chances of there being cockroaches (which is common in China) would be very slim. The housing agent was rushing me; we had only the weekend to find a place because the school authorities needed our home addresses to process our permanent resident visas. Fortunately, the company I was working at gave us the option of having a loan for 10,000 RMB to help us settle down. My rent cost 3,500 RMB; I had to pay first and last month's rent, and fifty percent of the rent as an agent fee to the housing agent. That came to a total of 8,750 RMB, so the loan came in handy, and 2,500 RMB was deducted from our pay check for the first four months. I signed a one year contract, and wait until you hear what happened next.

48-hour notice

The following story is very hard to believe. After six months of living in my apartment, the owner sent me a letter in Chinese and badly-written English, telling me that he has to sell his apartment in 48 hours, so I would have to vacate (I heard this happens very frequently in China to expatriates). Since I was oblivious to the culture and language, even though I had signed a one year contract, I complied on certain conditions before I released the keys to the apartment:

1- The owner should reimburse my first and last month deposit without penalty, for breaking the lease.
2- I would move out only on my day off.
3- I needed to be provided with a housing agent who speaks English well.
4- I could search for an apartment on my days off.

5- They needed to provide me with transportation because if I were to take a taxi, which would involve at least three trips, the taxi driver might take me north, south, east and west since he knew I am a foreigner. The cost would end up being exorbitant!
6- I needed an apartment at the same price, or less than what I was paying.
7- The apartment should be close to my job.

The housing agent took me to a building called 'Happiness Mansion' where many expatriates lived. He showed me five apartments which were more expensive than what I was paying, and they were not in good condition. They were cockroach-infested and needed re-painting. I declined all of them and then he had the effrontery to say to me, "You might want to look for another agent." I said, "Fine, no problem; there are other housing agents in Shenzhen." I began dialing my phone to call someone else, and he said, "Okay, let us look some more." (The agent thought I was going to beg him.) The sixth apartment was just right – it was the same price I was paying, and it was bigger and nicer! I shared this information with a friend, and she said she was given twenty days notice to move suddenly because the owner wanted to sell the apartment she was renting. I told her she had three weeks and I had two days, so her situation was not as bad as mine. I moved in on the 20th of the month, and my next water and electricity bills were very high. When I asked why they were so high, the building administrator said the previous tenant left and did not pay his bills, so I would have to pay his bill together with mine! I was very furious and called an interpreter, and the interpreter advised me to pay the whole bill even if part of it was not mine. "This is China. You will not win." As I had indicated in a previous chapter, if there is a conflict between a Chinese person and a foreigner, even if the latter was in the right according to Chinese law, preference would be given to the Chinese person. Because of this incident, of my refusal to pay the balance owing on utility bills from the previous tenant, the administration went to the extent of shutting the water valve so I was without water for a few days. I then paid the bill and my water was turned back on. After this incident, when I was about to return to Canada, I was advised by a Chinese friend not to tell the landlord, because they would bill me for my utilities at an exorbitant price, and, if I did not pay it, they would cut off my water and electricity before I leave. They will try to extort as much money from you as possible because the Chinese assume all westerners are very wealthy! The incidents with my apartments were indeed character building!

The saga of the Q-tip

The next incident is one I would not want my worst enemy to go through. It is the saga of the Q-tip. Shenzhen is an extremely hot city, and many times I could neither eat well, nor sleep well. If I left the air conditioner on all night, my electric bill would be very high. One very hot day, I woke up early at five a.m. because I could not sleep. I took my shower, and used a Q-tip made out of a wooden stem bought in China. Due to the extreme heat, there was much wax build-up so I

The Naked Educator

used force to clean my ears with the Q-tip. I suddenly heard a sound – Crack! I panicked and took out the Q-tip. I noticed the tip was stuck in my ear drum. I felt it was something easy to remove so I used a pair of tweezers to try to remove the Q-tip. Unfortunately, instead of it coming out, it went down my ear drum. Tears literally came out of my eyes. I hurried straight to the internet to read the consequences if the Q-tip edge was not removed. There were three:

1- It may cause hearing loss
2- It could cause dizziness
3- It may cause ear infection

Here I was at five a.m., in a foreign country, with a Q-tip lodged down my ear drum. I cannot speak Chinese and I could not remember the number for emergency. Whom could I call so early in the morning? I recall when I attended a Bible study; the facilitator introduced me to a medical student in her last semester who is now a medical doctor. He told me to exchange phone numbers with her because I may need her in the future. I decided to text her to see if she was awake, and luckily she was up. She told me not to panic and directed me to the closest hospital from where I lived, and said that she would meet me there. I got to the hospital and decided to take care of myself because she had already done a lot of interpretation for me. I had a sample Q-tip with me to demonstrate to the medical receptionist what happened. He understood my gestures and he wrote on a piece of paper the room number of the ear, nose and throat doctor. I went upstairs and met the doctor. She asked me in English, "How can I help you?" I related my story to her and she took an otoscope and looked in my ear. She saw the Q-tip piece and she asked me to sit still and close my eyes. Since I did not understand Chinese culture, I pretended to close my eyes and peeped. She was about to use a huge pair of tweezers and I screamed very loudly. She said to me, "That is why I asked you to close your eyes. If you want me to remove the piece of Q-tip, you need to remain still, and please do not move." I complied and she removed it and said to me, "You were lucky there was no ear damage." She advised me not to put Q-tips in my ears again, and that I should have my ears professionally cleaned. The saga of the Q-tip was another incident which, without any doubt, was a character-builder when I was in the Middle Kingdom.

Incident with an emergency physician

Another occurrence, which made me a stronger person, while in south east Asia, was when I had a medical emergency. One evening, at around eleven p.m., I had been hemorrhaging for three hours! This was not normal, and I did not have the emergency number by my bedside so I reached out to my close support group – my Bible study group via WeChat instant messenger. One of the Chinese men in my Bible study group, who speaks English very well, asked me to text him my address and he would send an ambulance to my place. John (his name has been changed for privacy) said he asked Mary (name changed for privacy) to meet me at the hospital where the ambulance would drop me off, and he would join us later. The ambulance came and the paramedics said, "Bring your money and passport." They took me in the ambulance, and when we got to the closest hospital, Mary met me there to do the necessary interpretation. John later joined her. When the emergency physician saw me, she said something in Chinese to John and Mary and they began laughing, and I asked what was funny. John told me that the doctor said, "I am scared, she is a foreigner." That means she is afraid of touching me; she does not want to be held liable if something were to happen to me. We then called the medical student for advice. She said that the ambulance should bring me to her hospital and she will talk to the doctor. An ambulance took me to another hospital thirty minutes away, and, in the meantime, I was going in and out of consciousness. Luckily for me, John and Mary accompanied me in the ambulance to help with interpretation. While in the ambulance, phones were passed back and forth for interpretation. I got to another hospital; the nurse cleaned me up and gave me an injection to stop the bleeding. By then I had lost a lot of blood and I was severely dehydrated, so I was given drips and I stayed on a very hard hospital bed all night in the hallway of the hospital. By then it was around one a.m., and Mary was giving me some water every thirty minutes. I asked Mary if she was a nurse and she said that she was an engineer, and she used to belong to my Bible study group. She and John stayed at the hospital by my bedside all night. She said her boss gave her permission to take the following day off from work. I was cold and Mary took off her coat and covered me, and John gave her his jacket. In the morning we all went for breakfast. This ordeal with the emergency physician occurred before I met my family doctor, my acupuncturist, my gynecologist and traditional Chinese medicine doctor.

Initial refusal to grant three-day medical leave

After my medical emergency, I was a given a prescription to take six injections, twice a day for three days, and also to have some bed rest. I emailed my supervisor stating that I needed to take three days off for medical reasons. I was shocked to hear him call me and say, "You cannot take three days off, we are short-staffed! You need to come in, and you can take your injection after work." Here I was, feeling very weak and on medication, and my supervisor (an expatriate himself) told me I had to come in to work. I said that I would. Things worked out later because he shared with one of my colleagues and she contacted me to hear what happened. Being a female, I was more comfortable sharing my story with her than with my male supervisor. She must have spoken to him afterwards; he later sent me an email saying that he had found a teacher from another center who would replace me while I was off for three days. I guess my colleague must have talked some sense into him. The whole incident was quite shocking, and I said to myself, "If I did not make it, would the school close down because they were short-staffed?" I think the answer is No!

Question and answer session with obstetrician/gynecologist

After a few months of living in China, my obstetrician/gynecologist advised me to have surgery, but I was neutral about the whole thing. She then asked me to come in with all the questions I had so she could answer all of them. These are the questions I asked her, which evidently built me up indirectly:

1-How many doctors will be doing the surgery?
2-How long has each of them been practicing?
3-How many hysterectomies have each of these doctors done?
4-Concerning blood transfusions, will I be able to use my own blood?
5-You mentioned earlier that my hospital stay will be two to three weeks. What facilities do they have in the room? For example, English television programs.
6-Can I use my cell phone in my room if I am hospitalized?
7- Does the hospital have Wi-Fi in the rooms?
8-Will I have a private room, or will I have to share with another patient?
9- Does the hospital have a nurse who does home visits after surgery?
10- You require someone to sign some papers on my behalf in case something happens. Does it have to be a family member, or can a friend do it?
11- If admitted, do I have to wear the hospital gown, or can I wear my own night clothes?
12-Does the hospital have nurses who speak English? Nina cannot

always be available, and it is not fair to always ask her to interpret for me.

13- What things are forbidden to have in hospital rooms in China?

14- You said that you recommend, if I decide to do the surgery, that I recuperate at home for three months. Is there any possibility of returning to work earlier?

15- With my surgery, will it precipitate menopause?

16- Will my cycle be less severe after the surgery?

17- After the surgery, what medications will I have to take, if any?

18- After the surgery, will I need to have any follow up visits?

19- Do you have any additional information from the last visit that I should send to my insurance?

20- Thank you for answering all my questions. Could you kindly fill out this portion of the insurance form for me please?

Taking a taxi

As simple as it may appear, taking a taxi was a big ordeal for me in China, and it certainly made me a stronger person. The first time I had to take a taxi was when I moved out of the Holiday Inn where the new expatriate teachers were lodged for two weeks. At the reception desk, I asked the hotel staff who spoke English to give me a ball point figure on how much it would cost to take me by taxi from the hotel to my new address, which I provided for them. They looked it up on the computer and said about 60-70 RMB. A taxi was waiting to pick up customers outside the hotel. I beckoned the driver to come inside the lobby and then I asked the hotel staff to ask the driver for a flat rate to my new address. The taxi driver said 100 RMB. The hotel staff spoke to me quietly that there is a rate for Chinese and a higher rate for expatriates, because Chinese people feel expatriates are wealthy. I told the hotel staff to tell him I will not pay 100 RMB. The driver said okay. I took the taxi and was watching the meter. When he came to my apartment, he was going around in circles, pretending as if he did not know the address. I told him and made a signal. Before getting out of the taxi, the amount was 65 RMB. He quickly changed the meter to 100 RMB. I shouted, took my things out, and gave him 65 RMB that was originally stated on the meter! From that day, while in China, I only took a taxi if I was with friends, or was returning late from an event and the subway was closed. I avoided taking taxis in Shenzhen. Apart from taking taxis in China, other things which built up my character were:

1- Pit latrine toilets with no bathroom tissue. Our Chinese colleagues said that when using pit latrine toilets, the advantage over the western ones is that all body waste is eliminated because our body is straight; but with western toilets, when sitting down, all body waste is not eliminated!

2- The passing of urine and feces on the street by babies and toddlers is very rampant. Chinese babies usually walk around with a split onesie and the grandparents, who usually look after their grandchildren, place their grandchildren on top of a garbage can on the street for them to answer nature's call.

3-The kinds of food the Chinese eat may not be palatable to some expatriates. For example, one day I went to the food court to buy some lunch because I had forgotten my lunch at home. I bought something I had seen in a beautiful photo displayed on the wall, but when I got it, it had an unusual odor. I went upstairs to the center and asked one of the Chinese teachers what it was. She laughed and said, We Chinese eat things that you westerners would never dream of eating." "Okay, good," I said, "But what is this that I bought please?" She laughed again and said, "It is coagulated pig's blood!" I thanked her for her honesty and discarded it when she left the office.

4- I cooked my own meals and brought my lunch and dinner to work, because we worked afternoons, evenings and weekends. All the Chinese staff expressed shock that I cooked my own meals. This really bothered me until I asked an expatriate teacher, who had lived in China for more than a decade, why they were so shocked. He said, "Because you are a foreigner, and the majority of foreigners do not cook, they eat out every day." I asked him where he got his statistics from. He said he had lived in China for a long time. He told me to start paying attention more and I will notice a trend. I asked two of my friends why they eat out daily, and they said it is cheaper to eat out and they do not have an adequate kitchen.

5- Many furnished apartments came without a cooking stove – maybe that was why many foreigners did not cook! These apartments also came without clothes dryers, unless you bought your own. The Chinese believe in drying clothes on a clothes line so the sun will touch the clothes for better health!

6- My apartment building was under construction and, since it was so hot, sometimes construction would be done at night when people were supposed to be sleeping.

7- When exiting or entering the subway, you have to watch out that you do not get trampled. Everyone just pushes.

8- Chinese people stare a lot at foreigners. I have a friend who is African-American. Her partner, a German, was married to a Chinese woman, and he has custody of the child. When all three of them are out together – a black woman and a white man, with a Chinese baby – they see confused looks on people's faces! They do not understand the mixture!

9-Chinese people do not have the concept of personal space like we have in the western world; they get right in your face. When I taught face to face classes in a small classroom of four students, I always had to move back, and I would explain to the students my reason for moving back. I educated them by telling them if you move too close to someone in the west, they will probably say, "You are in my personal space." I shared a joke with the students about a time when I was teaching in a college in Canada, and a student went right up to the instructor. He said to her, "You come so close to me, do you want to kiss me?" After I related the story, the students laughed.

From what has been discussed in the foregone paragraphs, after living in China for one year, it made me more appreciative of my country. Wait until you hear what part the power of faith has to play in my life in order to sustain my daily existence!

Chapter 7
The Power of Faith

Daily prayers

While I was in China, my prayer life improved drastically; I guess because I was in a foreign country where I was oblivious to both the language and the culture. I read my Bible daily and also read books such as *I Declare 31 Promises to Speak Over Your Life*, by Joel Osteen. For more information about this book, please visit my website at **thenakededucatorbook.com**. I also read books such as *The Law of Attraction*, by Martin Losier. These books, as well as many other books I read, kept my body and soul together. I also prayed on a daily basis that God would continue to strengthen me personally, physically, professionally and spiritually. When I enrolled in the TESOL (Teaching English to Students of Other Languages) course at the Global TESOL College in Toronto, Canada, the Director shared both positive and negative stories about foreign teachers in China. I really prayed that I would never encounter any problem with law enforcement officers. We were told police can stop a foreigner at any time and ask for their passport. Luckily, I kept photocopies with me in my purse at all times even if I were just going across the street to the grocery store. Fortunately, for me for the duration I was in China, I was never stopped by police for my passport. Every time I saw police, I would always say, "Ni hao," the Chinese version of hello. One day I was in the subway, and the police were stopping people and asking for their passports. I stood in line and said a silent prayer before I was about to give my passport, but the police looked at me and said, "Go, you always say 'Ni hao' to us, and you are always well-dressed; we know you have your passport with you!" Then I said, "Xie xie," which means thank you in English. Daily prayers cannot be done alone. To get the full benefit of your spiritual life, it has to be accompanied by Bible studies.

Bible studies

As I previously mentioned in chapter two, I taught mostly white-collar professionals in Shenzhen , China. Since we taught on weekends, I was unable to attend church on Sundays, unless a Chinese holiday fell on that day. As a result, I attended two Bible study groups on my days off, which were Wednesday and Thursday. One was held on Wednesday morning which had only female expatriates, while the other was on Thursday evenings with a mixture of men and women, Chinese and expatriates. The Bible study on Wednesday morning was more structured and we used books such as *The Inheritance* by Beth Moore, and *Wonder Struck – Awaken to the Nearness of God* by Margaret Feinberg. On the other hand, the Bible study on Thursday night was more informal. We had praise and worship, Bible reading and spiritual testimonies. At both Bible studies we brought refreshments and also socialized. While I was in China, I attended a regular church about five times because these days were Chinese holidays. There, I met a lady whose husband was a pastor, but was out of the country.

A pastor's wife's vision

While I was in China, I got to know a pastor's wife, and she and I became good friends. Ruth (name has been changed to protect her privacy) knew about my medical condition and she would pray for me often. Ruth told me she had a vision about me and that I should not opt for surgery. I have learnt from past experience that when a person of faith tells you not to do something, it is a good idea to obey. I will share a story pertaining to obedience to authorities which happened to me in Toronto, Canada. A few years ago I belonged to a cell group (Bible study group) and when it was time to go home, my cell leader told me not to go. She said, "Wait until my husband comes back home, then he will drop you at the bus stop." I said to her, "Magdalene, (name has been changed to protect her privacy) the bus stop is just two blocks away, I can walk." She insisted, and said, "No, do not go yet." We were trained in my church to obey spiritual leaders, for they see things that the lay person might not see. After about an hour and a half, Magdalene said, "My husband has not come yet, I think you can go." When I arrived at the bus stop, there was yellow tape sectioned out by the police. I asked someone what happened there and was told that there was a shooting about an hour and a half ago! That would have been about the same time I would have been at the bus stop. When I got home, I called Magdalene, my cell leader, and related the incident. She said, "That was why I asked you to stay; I saw that you might be embroiled in some kind of danger, so I used my husband dropping you as an excuse for you to stay in my home." There is a biblical allusion to this: *All of you must obey those who rule over you. There are no authorities except the ones God has chosen. Those who now rule have been chosen by God. So whoever opposes the authorities opposes leaders whom God has appointed (Romans 13:1).* For more information on spiritual leadership please visit my website at **thenakededucatorbook.com**.

To segue back to Ruth in China, the pastors' wife, being that it was a Chinese holiday and I was able to attend church, I asked her if we could fellowship after church and she said yes, so we went to her house which was quite far away. She was very happy to have a visitor since her husband was out of the country and she was left alone with her baby. She cooked some food, we ate, and she asked me to take the leftovers home. Strangely enough I was off for two consecutive Sundays so I could attend church again. The next Sunday I put out some turkey to thaw in the morning so when I returned from church, I could cook it. The Holy Spirit spoke to me that I should ask Ruth if she would like some frozen turkey. I called her and she began laughing. I asked her what was funny. She said, "I just finished my turkey last night, and I was praying that someone would give me some turkey because it is hard for me to go out shopping with a young baby." I think that was indeed a testimony which she shared on a Bible study Whatsapp conference call.

In addition to me attending Bible study groups, the pastor's wife held an online Bible study session with people from all around the world. People shared many testimonies which helped strengthen me, as well as others. A testimony is something which God has done for you, and sometimes you have been praying for a long time to obtain it. Testimonies are important because they can help another person. *They triumphed over him by the blood of the lamb and by the word of their testimony. (Revelations 12:11)*

English speaking Shekou Church

As I had mentioned earlier, I was unable to attend church regularly on Sundays because of my teaching schedule, but during the Chinese New Year and Christmas, I was able to attend church. The church rented out a space in a school gymnasium. If you did not come early, you would literally have to stand because all the chairs were taken. After a few months of me being in China, I was told the authorities gave them a deadline to move to another location. There were constant prayers by the congregation to find new accommodation. It is not easy to run English -speaking churches in China. They finally found a place in which to worship which was in a theater. The advantages of holding church in the theater were three-fold: 1- the congregation did not have to put away any folding chairs after church was over like they did in the previous church 2- There were more than enough seats so no one had to stand. 3- Everyone could see clearly because the theater was slanted from the top to the bottom. The protocol in this new location was so strict that members had to wear their name tags on lanyards, and visitors were given temporary name tags! Before exiting the church, someone was at the exit to keep the name tags for next week. I enquired why we had to wear name tags. Of all my years attending church, I had never seen people wearing name tags. I was advised they were wearing name tags for security reasons.

The church was a good church because each week a different person would preach to give a different flavor to the preaching. The congregation not only consisted of expatriates, but also local Chinese people, as well, who had converted into Christians.

Faith-based reading

While I was in the Middle Kingdom, I read *Growing in God's Favor* by Joel Osteen, on a daily basis. On the first of the month, I would read number 1, 11,21, 31, 41, 51, 61, 71, 81, 91 and 101, and then on the second day of the month I would read 2,22,32,42,52,62,72,82,92. These readings were done in addition to my Bible readings. Here are some excerpts from the book which had such a great impact on me spiritually that I deem it necessary to share it.

1-God wants us to go further. He never wants us to quit growing.

2-We should always be reaching for new heights in our abilities, in our spiritual walk, in our finances, careers and personal relationships. There are always new challenges, other mountains to climb, new dreams and goals that we can pursue.

3-When we are tempted to get negative and go around complaining, we need to just turn it around. We need to remember that God is in control.

4-If you will help somebody else become successful, God will make sure you are successful.

5-Look an obstacle in the eye and say, "I will defeat you. I am a child of the Most High God, and I am going to become all that He has created me to be."

6-God didn't create any of us to be average. He didn't make us to barely get by. We were created to excel.

7-You have seeds of greatness inside you, but it is up to you to believe and act on them.

8- God is constantly at work in your life. He is looking years down the road and getting everything perfectly in order, lining up solutions to problems you haven't even considered yet.

9-Your situation may seem unfair; it may be difficult. It may seem that forces working against you are winning momentarily, but God said He'd turn your circumstances around and use them to your advantage.

10-Get your song back. Say things such as, "Father, thank you for this day. Thank you that I'm alive." Every time you do that, God will fill you afresh with His joy, peace, strength, victory and favor.

11-You may have a big dream in your heart. Keep in mind that God may have put that seed in you to get it started. Your children and your grandchildren may take it further than you ever thought possible.
12-When the praises go up, the blessings come down.
13-In some battles, the only way you'll get out is to praise your way out. Don't fight with other people. Don't try to get even. Just stay full of praise, and God will fight your battles for you.
14-Quit looking at what's wrong. Quit talking about what didn't work out and start praising your way out.
15- You've got to shake off the discouragement. Shake off what didn't work out and start thanking God like you have already overcome. That's what faith is all about.
16- It's easy to get negative and lose our enthusiasm. But think about what the psalmist said – "I will keep on hoping for you to help me. I will praise you more and more."
17-God will never disappoint a praiser. Just ask Paul and Silas. At midnight, as they sang praises, God opened their prison doors. Just ask Daniel – as he gave God thanks, those hungry lions couldn't touch him. Just ask Shadrach, Meshach, and Abednego. They went into the fiery furnace full of praise and came out without even smelling like smoke.
18-When you stay in praise; you won't be able to out run the good things of God. Every time you turn around, you'll feel like it's raining His blessings.
19-When you get in a habit of bragging on God's goodness, you'll see Him do the extraordinary in your life.

20-All the forces of Heaven are backing you up. Dare to believe that you can become everything God has created you to be.

21-Psalm 81:10 says, "Open your mouth wide, and I will fill it with good things". One reason people never see God's best is because they barely have their mouths open. This is one time it's good to have a big mouth.

22- Start your day off by saying, "Father thank you that my best days are still out in front of me. Thank you that you've got favor in my future like I've never seen before."

23-God would not have put a dream in your heart if He had not already equipped you with what you need.

24-You know what a downpour is. It rains so hard, you can't see anything. That's what God wants to do in every one of your lives –pour out blessings that you cannot contain.

25-If we're going to experience God's favor, we've got to do our part and become favor minded.

26- There's something special about you. You've got the favor of God, and I'm not talking about being arrogant in thinking that you're better than somebody else. I'm talking about living with confidence because God is on your side.

27- You are a child of the Most High God. Your Father created the whole universe.

28- God wants you to have favor in everything you do and everywhere you go. The more you are aware of this favor, the more you're going to see it working in your life.

29-You've got to start expecting God's blessings to overtake you. Start expecting God's goodness to show up in your new life.

30-For too long, religion has beat people down, causing many to have the wrong image of God. They think He's mean. He's out to get them. But that's not the way our God is. God is a good God. (by Joel Osteen)

Joel Osteen wrote *101 of God's favor.* To read the remainder, please visit my website at **TheNakededucatorbook.com.**

The next chapter deals with a lot of positive things, so you need to continue reading.

Chapter 8
What I Liked About the Middle Kingdom

Entrepreneurial spirit of Chinese people

There were a number of things I liked about the Chinese. One of them was their business acumen. I usually travelled from Shenzhen to the mall in Guangzhou to have the beautician do my hair. Right next to the hairdresser was a Nigerian restaurant owned and operated by Chinese! I asked my hairdresser why a Chinese person was running a Nigerian restaurant. She related the story to me that a Nigerian man married a Chinese lady, and his wife asked the sister-in-law to teach her how to cook Nigerian food. When she learned the cooking methods, she taught other Chinese how to cook Nigerian food! This Nigerian restaurant was strategically located in "Chocolate City," also known as "Little Africa."

I met some ladies from the western world and they said many Chinese ladies have asked them to teach them how to do African braids, and they refused teaching them for fear that they may go out of business. Chinese people in general are involved in lots of businesses such as bakeries, restaurants, beauty suppliers and hotel proprietors.

I recalled, several years ago when I was teaching English in a college in Toronto, one Chinese student said, "Chinese people love money; they will do any business for money."

Dress code

Another aspect I liked about the Middle Kingdom is that the Chinese ladies like to dress formally. Some of them, in my center where I taught, dressed as if they were going to a party. Chinese women, unlike their western counterparts, do not show any cleavage. I made this remark to a friend who said, "How can they show something they do not have?" They do not have anything! For the one year I taught in China, I only saw one Chinese lady show her bosom. She was very obese and had a western partner.

Another part of their dress code I liked were the bank employees who wore black or navy blue suits with a white shirt and bow tie! From my opinion, they tend to be more conservative in their dressing. For example, many of them would wear shorts and have tights under them so as not to expose their hips.

Heath care professionals

In China, from what I observed, all health care practitioners wore medical masks when speaking to their patients. This was one way to distinguish them from the patients and also to avoid the spread of germs. Fortunately, medical masks are available at every reception counter and they were advertised free of charge to the public.

Efficient subways

What I liked about the subways in China were the enclosed solid glass doors to avoid anyone from jumping onto the railway tracks. At the end of each station, there is a solid glass acting as a barrier.

"In Chongqing, China, (Toronto's Chinese sister city) between now and 2020, plans to add more than 360 kilometers of road and railway to its public transit infrastructure." (Toronto Metro News, April 20, 2016). Let us juxtapose and examine the subway system of three Chinese cities:

Chongqing metro

"In Chongqing, China, the metro system consists of four lines and 120 stations. The system is undergoing a massive expansion and plans to have 18 lines and over 270 stations by 2050."

Hong Kong's public transit

"Hong Kong's public transit system is one of the most efficient and profitable systems in the world. The metro transit railway's fare box recovery ratio is 186 percent (the Toronto Transit Commission hovers around 70 percent), and it boasts a 99.9 percent on time rate for train time."

Shanghai metro system

"Shanghai Metro system is second only to Beijing in terms of ridership. An average of 10 million people use the system every weekday, and at 588 kilometers, it is the longest public transit network in the world!" (Metro News, April 20, 2016)

Other features about the subways I liked were the luggage x-ray machines and many security officers. Also, on a daily basis, there were janitors cleaning the subways.

Absence of guns

"Gun ownership in the People's Republic of China is heavily regulated by law. Generally, private citizens are not allowed to possess guns, and penalties for arms trafficking include death. Guns can be used by law enforcement, the military and paramilitary, and security personnel protecting property of state (including the arms industry, financial institutions, storage of resources, and scientific research institutions. The chief exception to the general ban for individual gun ownership is for the purpose of hunting. Illegal possession and sale of firearms may result in minimum punishment of 3 years in prison" [Wikipedia]. I

The Naked Educator

recall one expatriate saying that he felt safer in China than he did in his home country.

Senior citizens and Tai Chi

Every morning when I was going to work I would notice senior citizens on the grass performing Tai Chi with music playing nearby. Tai Chi is a Chinese martial art, and a form of stylized, meditative exercise, characterized by methodically slow circular and stretching movements and position of bodily balance. (www. Dictionary.com)

Free Wal-Mart bus ride

One thing which I liked very much while living in Shenzhen was the availability of a free Wal-Mart bus, taking us back and forth. I stumbled on this bus by accident. While I was about to board bus 80 to Wal-Mart, I noticed a Wal-Mart bus pull up behind it and people got in.

I decided to enter the bus and I asked, "Is there anyone here who speaks English?" Luckily, a man from Hong Kong replied, "Yes, I speak English, how can I help you?" I said, "Can anyone enter this bus, and how much is it?" The man said, "Anyone can enter this bus; it is free, and do not tip the driver, otherwise it would be regarded as an insult!" Welcome to China! If you are taking this bus back home, show the driver your Wal-Mart receipt and tell him where to drop you. I thanked the man for his assistance. I later on found out that this Wal-Mart bus was actually provided free of charge to expatriates who lived at the Peninsular, but Chinese people started using it as well.

The posh peninsular neighborhood

The Peninsular is a posh neighborhood in Shekou, Shenzhen where mostly expatriates live. It is a narrow piece of land projected into the sea and has a romantic scenery. There were a number of western stores which catered to the needs of expatriates. The wet market was also nearby and I used to shop there after Bible study. A wet market is a market selling fresh meat, fruits and vegetables, distinguished from dry markets which sells durable goods such as clothes and electronics. The prices here at the wet market were cheaper than those in the store.

Nogogo online groceries

"Nogogo is your one-stop online shop for imported groceries and goods that can be ordered online from the comfort of your home or office and delivered to your door! The business started with a craving with one of the founding members not being able to purchase the products he wanted. Why the name Nogogo? It's easy to remember! You don't need to go; we go to you." (www.nogogo.cn)

Some Australians were very wise to start a grocery and delivery store containing foreign food to cater to the expatriate community. The products are expensive, but, in the long run, if one was really craving for imported food, one could have it delivered at your home or your office.

SeaWorld

Just as the Peninsular is a posh neighborhood where expatriates live, SeaWorld is an area in Shenzhen where one could find many western restaurants and businesses. There are Italian, Mexican, American, Greek restaurants and western bars. There is also a very big, white, beautiful stationary ship which hosts a posh hotel and restaurants. When I planned an event for teachers, I took them to one of the restaurants in SeaWorld and they loved the atmosphere. It is very romantic at night with beautiful water cascades. No expatriate lives in Shenzhen without going to SeaWorld!

Elementary school children and Physical Education

When I first arrived in Shenzhen for the two weeks I stayed at the Holiday Inn hotel, I noticed elementary school children on the school field doing physical education for about one hour before school began. This was accompanied by some loud music, but it was good music.

Keeping in shape can help your child throughout her life.

10 Benefits of Physical Activity by Karin A. Bilich
1-It strengthens the heart.
2- It helps keep arteries and veins clear.
3-It strengthens the lungs.
4-It reduces blood sugar levels.
5-It controls weight.
6- It strengthens the bones.
7-It helps prevent cancer.
8- It regulates blood pressure.
9- It provides energy levels.
10-It enhances emotional well-being.
For a more detailed version of these benefits please visit my website at **thenakededucatorbook.com**.

Free Chinese lessons

Western teachers were given the opportunity to have free Chinese lessons. The classes were held once a week and were facilitated by Chinese teachers who taught English in the center. Luckily the classes were not mandatory, for I was not interested at all in learning the language. After what I had gone through, I did not foresee myself living in China for more than a year, so I did not want to waste my time because I did not see it as beneficial to me at that time.

The Naked Educator

All said and done, it was a good idea to have Chinese lessons. There were also some free online classes available as well for those interested. From time to time, Chinese students would be brought into the classrooms to assist the teachers with their pronunciation. I did not want any student making fun of me, so learning Chinese at the center did not interest me at all.

Another option was to have a private tutor. I knew two students at my center who used to teach Chinese to expatriates for a fee of 200 RMB ($40 Canadian).

Re-writing official documents

While I was in China, I wired money every month via western union and I had to fill out some paper work at the bank. The Chinese policy is that if you make a mistake, you cannot initial it and continue like it is done in the western world. The bank personnel will request you re-write the entire form. Even if it means to re-write it several times!

The warm climate

The best thing I liked about Shenzhen was the warm weather. That was one criterion I used to choose the city to teach in. I understood from my research, and from talking to some Chinese people, that Beijing, the capital, and Shanghai, the commercial and financial city located in the north, can be very cold. I chose Shenzhen to escape the brutal Canadian cold weather. In Shenzhen, there was hardly any winter and absolutely no snow. In fact, it got so hot that if I did not drink sufficient water, I started feeling dizzy!

Because of the extreme heat, during my last three months there, I lost ten pounds, and some of my students noticed my weight loss. The next chapter deals with some takeaways of the Naked Educator.

Chapter 9
Life Lessons Learned

A better interpreter

One important lesson I learned was being a better interpreter. I was a community accredited French interpreter for one year prior to going to China. I took a one year leave of absence and upon my return, I resumed my duties as an interpreter. When I was in China, the roles were reversed. I was the client and I needed an interpreter. Today I am more empathetic, compassionate and understanding. Also, I am an extremely good listener, have excellent sensory, motor and cognitive skills. All of these skills need to work in unison to ensure that not only language, but all nuances and idioms are picked up on and relayed in a comprehensive way, all in the blink of an eye! I am more culturally-aware. Just as specialist subject knowledge is very important, I am more aware of the culture of the languages, I am more aware of the source and target languages. I am now more able to cope with stress and self-control when dealing with difficult speakers. Not everyone speaks with precision and clarity, and of course accents can be difficult to discern. Interpreters need to keep their cool and remain relaxed, even in seemingly tough situations. Returning from China, I am more emotionally resilient. I do legal and medical interpreting which are sometimes cases that are high profile or difficult to witness, such as emergency medical situations. In such instances, I have to show high levels of resilience and control with the people I am there to represent. (*The 6 Qualities of a Good Interpreter, The Language Factory*)

Dress code for Chinese women

Chinese women, as I had discussed earlier, do not show their cleavage like how many women in the west do. The Chinese are more conservative in their dressing, and maybe some expatriates in the western world could copy this good habit.

Remembering our differences

Expatriates who teach in the Middle Kingdom should remember our differences. We (expatriates) can learn a lot from the Chinese, and vice versa.

Travel prior to a holiday

One lesson learned while I was in China is NEVER to travel out of the city the day before a holiday. I made the mistake of going to Guangzhou, and upon return I went to the train station there and all the train tickets were sold out! I was stranded in Guangzhou and my battery on my phone was dead, and I had forgotten my charger in

Shenzhen. What was I going to do? I had such a long day that I collapsed on the floor, and, of course, unable to speak Chinese, I just lay on the floor. I got up later, and not knowing what to do, just paced the rail way station. Suddenly a man asked me, "Shenzhen?" I said, "yes." He told me to give him money, and I declined. He beckoned me to follow him and I noticed there was a bus taking people to Shenzhen. As a result of the train tickets being sold out, the price of the bus tripled! I paid and got onto the bus. I met some Chinese who spoke English, and they told me to come and sit with them. They advised me never to travel the day before a holiday because of the amount of travelers.

Credit card ordeal

One lesson learned while I was in China was my ordeal with my Canadian credit card. Before leaving Canada, I informed my financial institution that I would be away in south east Asia for one year. They told me my credit card would be cancelled after two months because they were afraid that because I am so far away, I might default on my payment. I then asked my bank how they handle credit cards for snow birds. They told me they are allowed to go for six months and return to their home country, or else their credit cards will be cancelled.

The importance of face in Chinese culture

"If you have spent any time around Chinese culture, you have come across the idea of losing face."

"Losing face," and "saving face," are ideas often used in western cultures, but Chinese culture brings face to a whole new complicated level. Here is an example. A local youth invited a few English teenagers to participate in a series of games to celebrate the end of the term. Everyone in the activity was split into groups. There was a team made up of teenage students, a team of foreign English teachers, a parent's team, and a team of Chinese teachers. Everything started out lightheartedly, and each team took turns winning at a variety of relay races, but, during one event, everything quickly changed. One of the last races required the teams to use chopsticks to carry a Ping-Pong ball across the finish line. Players had to switch the ball from player to player, but they were not allowed to touch or drop the ball. The other team laughed at the idea of foreigners even having a chance to win at the event. The foreigners decided to focus and show just how good their chopsticks skills were.

The race began, and our team quickly went in to the lead. After the first two switches, we knew that our team of foreigners was going to win by a long distance. Soon, all the good-natured laughter had stopped. The other teams were not even cheering anymore. Unfortunately, we did not notice the lack of excitement until we crossed the finish line. The other teams vied for second place in awkward silence.

After the race, some of the students congratulated us, but none of the parents, or Chinese teachers, would even look in our direction. A student finally told us that we had caused the adults to lose face by not just winning, but also by defeating them by such a large margin. I asked why it mattered, as we had won a different competition before. The student explained that we were not supposed to be good at using chopsticks, because that was a Chinese skill.

Losing face in Chinese culture is about more than being embarrassed. In Chinese culture, you spend your entire life trying to build social prestige and reputation, while also trying to avoid causing anyone else to lose theirs. You gain face, less by individual achievement, and more by promoting social harmony and being seen as helpful. Face is closely tied to relationships. When you lose face it means your ability to function as part of the social order has been damaged. You have lost influence and injured your reputation." (www.yoyochinese.com)

Western versus Eastern notions of face

"Westerners, especially Americans, grow up with the idea that life and business are zero-sum competitions: some win and most lose. Most Asian cultures are built on more of a Confucian notion of social harmony and strict hierarchy.

Chinese game shows and sporting events often go to what seem like extreme efforts to avoid having losers, or to keep losers from feeling shamed or embarrassed.

When our team of foreigners won by such a large margin, we disrupted social harmony in the worst way.

"We showed up the teachers and parents in front of their students and children. Their reputations as the source of Chinese cultural value was tarnished because we beat them at a particularly Chinese contest of skill. After embarrassing our hosts, we were never invited back to any extra-curricular activities with our students." (www.yoyochinese.com)

"The modern concept that ties face to the idea of honor and reputation is clearly related to the ideas of Confucianism, but it is impossible to find the exact origin of the concept of face in Chinese culture. Whatever the source, there is no doubt that complicated efforts to save face are part of every Chinese relationship, from business to politics, from friendships to families.

Westerners can easily misinterpret the idea of face as Chinese people simply being too sensitive or thin skinned. But, in reality, face is a complicated part of good manners in China. Failure to understand face may result in awkward situations and burned bridges.

The untrained observer might miss the importance of face in different social situations. When Chinese job seekers are interviewed for a position, employers will not tell them at the interview that they did not get the job. This would cause the employee to lose face. Job seekers are also eager to show employers that they will be valuable assets, but not valuable enough to replace their bosses. Humility is one of the key factors in getting a job with a Chinese employer. Foreigners will have more friends, and have better luck in business, if they learn to show humility in public, and to allow saving face in awkward situations and business deals. If you can change your focus from winning to preserving harmony, it is much easier to get along in China." (www.yoyochinese.com)

Why teach abroad

" Whether you are a seasoned professional teacher or someone just finishing university studies, you have probably imagined yourself in a far-off land where the pace of life is slower, more relaxed, and where fresh discoveries await you at every turn. Teachers of English are in especially high demand, with an estimated one billion people worldwide waiting to learn English. The range of opportunities abroad for teachers and school administrators runs the gamut, from private English language schools, to international and American schools, NGO-sponsored positions, universities, technical institutions, multinational firms, professional organizations, religious schools, and teaching private lessons for a few weeks or months while travelling. Assignments range from a couple of months to three years or more." *Teaching Abroad – The Big Guide to Teaching and Working Overseas, Fourth Edition* by Jean-Marc Hackey.

Educators are in the enviable position of being able to use work for travel-learning experiences. Going abroad may be a way to enhance your career or get into the education field, a chance to see a part of the world that has always appealed to you, have an adventure, make new friends, rejuvenate a career that has gone stale, do some humanitarian work or simply earn an honest living.

On a professional level, teachers who work overseas almost always find new enthusiasm and a fresh outlook on their subject area and their careers. A successful experience in another culture results in greater confidence in your own teaching ability.

The qualities of a teacher working abroad

"Making final decisions takes courage and enthusiasm. For some, teaching abroad can be tremendously disruptive. Experienced international teachers, on the other hand, think nothing of giving up their possessions, renting out their homes for a year or two, and freeing themselves of the worries of retirement and savings. They have a realistic understanding of loneliness and homesickness. Overseas teachers see themselves as free spirits and risk takers, able to pick up and move themselves, and, in many cases, their families to each new posting with enthusiasm, anticipation and curiosity."
Qualities of a Teacher Working Abroad, the Big Guide to Teaching and Working Overseas

Seven lessons learned while teaching in China

Teaching abroad is a wonderful way to expand your comfort zone, experience a new culture and get some great teaching experience. You will learn a lot about yourself and your teaching style, and there will be some special moments that you could not have anywhere else.

1-The teacher is sometimes the student.

2-My job is not to give answers, but to start a conversation that my students can continue on their own time.

3-People tend to view me as brave and/or lucky.

4-There will be frustrating moments.

5-Not every moment has to be geared toward personal and professional development.

6-Sometimes things will get lost in translation.

7-You cannot beat those smiles.

(Seven Life Lessons I Learned While Teaching in China by Jess Signet, February 4, 2016)

Chapter 10
Suggestions for Surviving in the Middle Kingdom

The title of my book is *The Naked Educator,* and the reason for such a catchy phrase is to share with readers my innocence going into China. Any educator and university or college graduate in their gap year should take heed of the advice in this chapter, which happens to be the most important chapter in the book. Pay attention to the following advice to make your stay in China more enjoyable and meaningful.

Pre-departure check list

1a-If you own a house or condo, and you plan to rent it out, do not rent it out until you are one hundred percent sure you have your Chinese visa, and your airline ticket with a fixed date, not a tentative date. In my case, I was left stranded without a place to stay because I rented out my condo, and, later, my expected arrival date was changed because my recruiter fell ill and went on medical leave. My arrival date was postponed from September 6, 2014 to October 22, 2014. I rented my condo for September 1, 2014, so technically I did not have a place to stay from August 31 to October 22. Please do not make a similar mistake. I was then obliged to stay with two friends; one for four weeks, and the other for three weeks!

b-Visit a travel medical clinic and get the necessary prescription medications where applicable.

c-Make sure you have a current passport before filling out your application form to teach in China. Also do not let it expire while you are away from your home country. I renewed my passport for ten years before travelling to the Middle Kingdom.

2- As soon as you obtain your home address, register with the embassy of your country, so that in times of emergency such as evacuation, you will be accounted for and your next of kin will be notified.

3- Carry your passport with you at all times. Decide whether to carry the actual passport or photocopies. There are advantages and disadvantages in carrying the passport or photocopies. Let me share with you two stories I heard happened in Shenzhen. A few years ago, police visited a language center and asked all the expatriate educators for their passports. All twenty of them produced photocopies of their passports. The police would not accept their photocopies and whisked them all to the local police station. They were interrogated and detained. The visa officer for the school in question was called and she spoke to the police, but the police insisted on them having their passports with them. She came to the police station, got the addresses of all the teachers and the location in their apartments where their passports could be found, and then she had to go into their apartments to retrieve their passports. After she returned with all their passports, the instructors were then released. On the flip side of this story, another teacher went to a conference and afterwards went out with some friends to a nearby lounge and left his clutch, which contained his passport in it on a stool. At the same time, a beggar was passing, asking each of them for money. When it was time to go home, he realized that his clutch had disappeared! It cost him thousands of RMB (renminbi- Chinese currency), equivalent to hundreds of dollars to replace his passport.

4- As soon as you get your Chinese address, write it down in both English and Chinese, place in your wallet, program it into your phone and place it by your bedside in case of an emergency. If you want to take a taxi home, just show the address to the taxi driver.

5- Learn how to use chopsticks properly, or else have some silverware with you in a Ziploc bag in your handbag. Some restaurants do not carry silverware, except the high-end ones.

6-In case of a medical emergency, have a backup plan and also have the emergency numbers by your bedside, in your wallet and also programmed in your phone – 120 is for ambulance, 110 is for police and 119 is for firefighters.

7-Learn as much of the Chinese culture and language as possible. It will make your life more enjoyable and meaningful.

8-When you leave your country of origin for China, make sure to extend your health coverage, so in case of a medical evacuation or if you go on holidays, your health coverage is still valid.

9- Be tolerant of the Chinese culture, for some of the things done, you will not agree with. They also may not agree with what foreigners do and say.

10-Mattresses in China are very hard. The Chinese claim it is good for the back, so what I did was to buy a foam mattress to put on top of it.

11- Some people originating from other countries are accustomed to tipping, but in China tips are not given in restaurants, for it is regarded as an insult.

12- Some people wear medical masks on the streets for reasons such as pollution or a bad cough.

13- Many Chinese people stare a lot at foreigners, especially if you are tall. They stare due to curiosity. I handle the staring by saying, "Ni hao ma" (Mandarin for "How are you doing?"), and waving and smiling.

14- Always have sanitary towelettes or sanitizing gel and bathroom tissue with you to use in public washrooms.

15- I lived in Shenzhen in the south east of China which was so hot that my suits had some white mildew while they hung in my closet. This was due to the humidity, so I solved the problem by placing a bowl of water in my closet.

16- Always have an exercise book and pen in case you want to write down or draw something, if you cannot speak Chinese.

17- The banks are very strict when exchanging money. If your tender bills are torn, they will not accept them. All you need to do is to go to a foreign exchange bureau and they will be accepted.

18- When teaching in a language center you can be transferred anytime to another one due to shortage of educators.

19- When you move into a new apartment, the owner will change the locks which the tenant has to pay for. Do not give the owner a copy of your keys, or they will access your apartment at any time without warning.

20- Some Chinese interpreters do not interpret everything you tell them. For instance, I had an issue of the building staff entering my apartment without any warning. When I lodged a complaint through an interpreter, I sensed the sentence was not interpreted correctly. I asked the interpreter if he told her what I said. He admitted by saying, "We Chinese do not talk like that, so I did not interpret what you said".

21-Some public toilets have western-style toilets, while others have pit latrines. You can tell availability of both kinds by looking at the pictures on the door.

22- I heard of a story of an expatriate educator who found an apartment and liked everything. The only thing she did not like was the pit latrine. To solve the situation, she bought a portable western toilet and placed it over the pit latrine!

23-As I had discussed earlier, the Chinese have high business acumen. One kind of public transportation used is the motor bike taxi. You are riding at your own risk because there is no law to wear a helmet!

24-When traveling by bus or train out of the city, you will need your passport as a form of identification in order to purchase tickets.

25-Many Chinese men tend to carry their female partner's handbag when out in public. I understand that is their own way of being romantic and caring. Do not be shocked by this gesture which might appear strange to some foreigners.

26- According to Chinese law, if a foreigner and Chinese have a dispute, and law enforcement is involved, favoritism will be given to the Chinese, even if the foreigner is right.

27- If an educator gets romantically involved with another educator or student, the educator will be asked to transfer to another center. Another alternative is resignation.

28-If you are a tall expatriate and you want to buy large clothes, they may be hard to find because the Chinese in general are small people. There are three choices: buy the clothes in Guangzhou or Hong Kong, or have clothes sewn by a tailor.

29-Never drink water directly from the tap. I bought a kettle, boiled the water, and drank it when it was cool.

30- According to Chinese norms/mores, they cure their illnesses by drinking hot water. When I was in China, my favorite drink was sliced lemon with warm water which helped alkalize my body. For further information on how to survive in China, please read the Guide to Living in China located on my website at **thenakededucatorbook.com**.

31-Beware of your surroundings even if you do not speak Mandarin. Take cues from others. For example, one day there was an announcement made in Mandarin. The train stopped suddenly; I noticed everyone disembarked from the train, and I followed.

32- If you are craving to read a book written in English, you can find them in specialty shops in the big cities such as Hong Kong, Beijing, Shanghai and Shenzhen.

33- Always keep some water in a big bottle or jug in your apartment in case of water shortage.

34- Chinese people tend to ask many personal questions, so use tact and diplomacy when answering them.

35-In some Chinese apartments, instead of having a bolt on the door there is a secondary door made out of steel! This is for security.

36-Sometimes, when a foreigner alights from a train or bus, some Chinese cover their nostrils as they pass each other. Just ignore them; it could be your perfume they do not like.

37-Whenever you have anything sent to China by snail mail, always have it registered with a signature upon receipt. It is also wise to send it to your work address.

38- Many Chinese students like taking photos of food, and also with their foreign English-speaking teachers. These photos are usually advertised on WeChat, a Chinese messaging application. It is a way of bonding with their teachers and showing off to their friends that they are studying English.

39-If you do not like doing house chores or cooking at home, hire an "ayi," a Chinese maid who is relatively inexpensive.

40-I understand everything in China is recyclable except human beings!

41- When teaching Chinese students, speak slowly and audibly for better comprehension.

42- When opting for surgery in China, they require a family member or next of kin to sign medical documents.

43-Use both hands when giving paper tender bills and business cards; if not, you will be regarded as rude.

44-In China, expatriate educators are often asked to pay for their internet for the whole year.

45- I had a television set which came furnished with the apartment;

however, it was not set up due to the exorbitant rates, and very few English channels. I lived for one year without a television. We visited another expatriate who had CNN on his television. He said his apartment came with a television package. It is possible to live in China without a television.

46- Facebook, as well as other social media, are banned in China. In addition to this, Gmail and Google are also banned. However, Facebook is allowed in Hong Kong. To overcome this ban, some westerners subscribe to a VPN (virtual private network) for one year.

47-If you are a female instructor, and you are tall and obese, have a conservative hair style. I heard of a story of a foreign female teacher who was robust. She had a big Afro hair style, and, when she entered the classroom for the first time, one of the children began crying. Luckily, there was a Chinese teacher assistant in the classroom who observed and went to ask the child why she was crying. She said the new teacher's hair was so big, she was scared.

48- If you are a tall teacher, while teaching in China, as well as other Asian countries, to appear less intimidating, you may want to sit down occasionally.

49-In China, as an educator, I was advised by the Center Education Manager (my supervisor), never to write the names of students with a red pen because this is associated with death.

50- Also do not give anyone a clock, a watch or anything depicting time as a gift, because they are associated with death.

51- Be careful when walking on the street so as not to step on dog waste. Some owners inadvertently forget to pick it up.

52- There tends to be a lot of pollution in China; the bigger the city, the more the pollution. I have seen instances when I went for a pedicure and there was no sink in the room, and the esthetician just threw the dirty water out on the street. One way to combat some pollution is to wear a medical mask on your face while out on the street.

53-When taking a taxi in China, always ask for a " fapiao," which means receipt, so if you forget something in the taxi, it can be retrieved later.

54-As an expatriate, be careful what you say and do, for you could be thrown in jail, or be killed. I read of a foreign teacher who was thrown in a Chinese jail for three years. When he returned to his country, his family thought he was dead because they had not heard from him in three years.

55- The number 8 has long been regarded as the luckiest number in Chinese culture. With the pronunciation of 'Ba' in Chinese, number 8 sounds similar to the word "Fa," which means make a fortune. It contains meanings of prosperity, success and high social status too, so all business men favor it very much. People with the lucky number 8 have strong intuition and insight, so they have the potential to explore things undiscovered. Now I understand why some of the Chinese students and counselors came to me for advice! My birth date happens to be number 8, and everyone knew the birthday of the foreign teachers! To illustrate how highly the number 8 is prized, the telephone number 8888-8888 was sold for a sum corresponding to USD $270,723 in Chengdu, the capital of China's Sichuan province. Even the Chinese government got caught up in the euphoria over the number 8 in this Olympic year, 2008: the opening ceremony of the Summer Olympics in Beijing began on the eighth of August (08/08/08), at precisely 8 minutes and 8 seconds past 8 p.m., local Beijing time! (www.chinatravel.com)

56- On the other hand, the numbers four and fourteen are omitted in some Chinese buildings. Number four is considered an unlucky number because it is nearly homophonous to the word "death". The four is pronounced "si" in Chinese, the same as death.

57- Through conversation with my Chinese friends, I learnt that there is an occupation known as mistress negotiator! A man could have a wife in Beijing and a mistress in Shanghai. If a divorce occurs, the mistress negotiator will decide how many of the assets the mistress will inherit!

58-As I mentioned in an earlier chapter, Chinese people, as well as other Asians, are accustomed talking to each other at a very close distance. Politely just move back, or turn sideways, so that you can be more comfortable and the individual will not be violating your personal space.

59-If you want to live among taller Chinese, they are usually located in the northern part of China such as in cities like Beijing, the capital and Shanghai, the commercial and financial center of mainland China.

60- As a foreign educator teaching English in China, it is a good idea to wire money to your home country on a monthly basis when you get paid, be it the USA, Canada, the UK, Australia, New Zealand, or Ireland. This money will come in handy when you decide to go on vacation, or if, and when, you return permanently. Also, have a joint account with someone in your home country so if something were to happen, you still have access to your money.

61. One of the banks which has a western union is called ABC Agricultural Bank of China. If you want to wire money from your Chinese bank to your home bank, it is a more complicated process as a foreigner. But it is easier for a local Chinese to do the bank transfer.

62- Many educators, when they come to China to teach, to avoid loneliness, decide on having another expatriate as a roommate. Some of the roommates work out and some do not, just like anywhere in the world. Note, if you sign a one year lease and your roommate decides to leave, say after six months, you are stuck with the whole rent until you can find a replacement, which might not be right away.

63- Either obtain one year's supply of your prescription medications from your home country or else remember to write down the names, purpose and dosage of all your medications, so that you can obtain the equivalent while in China.

64- In some language schools, foreign teachers are paid once a month, a few days before their Chinese counterparts. Since you are only paid once a month, unlike every two weeks as we are accustomed to in the western world, you need to budget accordingly.

65- If you can change your focus from winning to preserving harmony, it is much easier to get along in China. Status in China is less about self-aggrandizement, and more about your relationship with others. If you can be gracious and humble in China, all kinds of doors will be open to you, even as a foreigner.

66- Chinese people are curious when they see foreigners. Sometimes you can be sitting in the train or bus, and they touch your hair because they admire it. How I handled it was to tilt my head the opposite way and make a sign not to do it. I do not make a scene because, remember, I mentioned earlier that if a foreigner and a Chinese have a dispute, the Chinese will be favored over the foreigner.

67. It is highly recommended, if possible, when coming to teach in China, to come with a partner. Reason being that it is cheaper for the company. For example, if a couple came together, the company will pay for only one hotel room instead of two rooms when they first arrive, thereby saving money. Another aspect is the apartment. The housing agent will look for one apartment instead of two apartments, and you can get a larger place since you are both sharing the cost. In the long run, it is a win-win situation.

68- Have a translation app on your mobile phone, especially when you want to go shopping. If you cannot find the item you are looking for, just type the English name into your phone and it will give you the Chinese equivalent. A good one which I used is called I-translate.

69- Another option when going grocery shopping, if I cannot find what I want, I go to Google images and print a picture and show the sales assistant, and they show me where the items are found.

70- There is an age limit to apply for a Chinese working visa: it is 55 years for women and 60 for men. There are some exceptions in certain cases.

71- Due to the extreme heat in certain cities, when it is very hot Chinese people open their umbrellas and walk under them in the streets. At first expatriates found that strange, but afterwards westerners began doing it also.

72- Keep a very open mind while in China.

Personal Disclaimer:

The above-mentioned are a few suggestions on how to survive in The People's Republic of China. If I have offended anyone in any way, it is not intentional. This is merely my own personal story. This information was mostly derived from observation, speaking to Chinese students/colleagues as well as through reading. Also, I shared ideas with an expatriate educator who has lived in China for sixteen years! If you decide to come and teach in the Middle kingdom, you may or may not experience what I went through in my one year journey from October 2014 to October 2015, in the most populated country, the People's Republic of China.

My book is a guide to help new educators or college and university graduates in their gap year going to China to teach, to avoid many mistakes I made. My experience there made me a stronger woman, professionally, personally and spiritually.

REFERENCES

Bilich, Karin. *10 Benefits of Physical Activity*

British Council. *Teaching English*

Cao, Emily; Mcnally,Jennifer; Niamh,Ryan; Song,Amber; Thorburn, Ross; Wang, Lillian; Wilkes, Laura; Zhao, Anna. *Guide to Living in China*

Canfield, Jack. *The Law of Attraction*

Flanagan, Alice; Zurikina, Svetlana; Labbo, Linda. *Chinese New Year*

Lyceum Books, Inc. *How to Teach Effectively*

Marc, Jean. *Teaching Abroad. The Big Guide to Teaching and Working Overseas*

Marc, Jean. *Qualities of a Teacher Working Abroad.* The Big Guide to Teaching and Working Overseas.

Newman, Jacqueline. *Food Culture in China*

Osier, Martin. *The Law of Attraction*

Osteen, Joel. *I Declare: 31 Promises to Speak over Your Life*

Osteen, Joel. *101 of God's Favor*

Signet, Jess. *Seven Lessons I learned While Teaching in China.* February 4, 2016

Simcoes, Luke. *Mayor Tory Praises Transit in Asia on return to Toronto.* Toronto Metro. Wednesday, April 20, 2016

The Cultural Factor. *Why do Chinese People Eat with their Mouths Open?* April 4, 2013

The Language Factory. *The 6 Qualities of a Good Interpreter*

Walker,Tracey. *21-day Blogging Challenge*

Wei, Liming. *Chinese Festivals*